Tools of the Mammoth Hunters

The application of use-wear analysis on the Czech Upper Palaeolithic chipped industry

Andrea Šajnerová-Dušková

BAR International Series 1645

2007

Published in 2016 by
BAR Publishing, Oxford

BAR International Series 1645

Tools of the Mammoth Hunters

ISBN 978 1 4073 0079 5

BAR Publishing is the trading name of British Archaeological Reports (Oxford) Ltd.
British Archaeological Reports was first incorporated in 1974 to publish the BAR
Series, International and British. In 1992 Hadrian Books Ltd became part of the BAR
group. This volume was originally published by Archaeopress in conjunction with
British Archaeological Reports (Oxford) Ltd / Hadrian Books Ltd, the Series principal
publisher, in 2007. This present volume is published by BAR Publishing, 2016.

Printed in England

BAR
PUBLISHING

BAR titles are available from:

BAR Publishing
122 Banbury Rd, Oxford, OX2 7BP, UK
EMAIL   info@barpublishing.com
PHONE   +44 (0)1865 310431
FAX   +44 (0)1865 316916
www.barpublishing.com

Contents

Preface v

1. Introduction to the method and history of use-wear analysis 1

    1.1 Traceology versus typology 5

    1.2 Interpretative possibilities and limits of the method 7

2. Material and Methods 11

    2.1 Artefacts 11

    2.2 Experiments 12

    2.3 Technical equipment 13

    2.4 Data registration 14

    2.5 LPA 15

    2.6 HPA 15

    2.7 Common variables 16

    2.8 Cleaning 16

    2.9 Postdepositional modification 17

3. Pavlov I (excavation 1954, 1957, 1970-71) 21

    3.1 Material and sampling 22

    3.2 Results and discussion 23

    3.3 Conclusion 29

4. Dolní Věstonice II-A (excavation 1999) 41

    4.1 Material and sampling 41

    4.2 Results and discussion 42

    4.3 Conclusion 44

5. Stránská Skála III 49

    5.1 Material and sampling 50

    5.2 Results and discussion 50

    5.3 Conclusion 52

6. The late Upper Palaeolithic and Mesolithic settlement of the karstic areas 59

    6.1 Material and sampling 59

    6.2 Results and discussion 60

    6.3 Conclusion 61

7. Discussion: Function, morphology and settlement 65

    7.1 Hafting 65

    7.2 Scrapers 66

    7.3 Burins 68

    7.4 Blades and flakes 70

    7.5 Points 73

    7.6 Microliths 74

    7.7 Settlement type and a degree of development of use-wear traces 75

    7.8 Contribution of LPA and HPA to the functional interpretation 77

8. Conclusion 79

Acknowledgements 81

References 83

Preface

Moravia played a very important role in the Palaeolithic migration of the ancient Homo sapiens as it made a natural corridor between the South and the North of the Middle Europe, which allowed for shifting of both humans and animals in times of glaciations. This fact is amply evidenced by a dense net of Palaeolithic settlements. In order to obtain the best information about the life during the Palaeolithic on the territory of Moravia, extensive researches have been performed since the beginning of last century. However, the method of use-wear analysis has recently been introduced into Czech researches.

A program of research of the functional analysis of Palaeolithic stone tools was undertaken between 1999 and 2005 at the Hrdlička Museum of Man, Charles University in Prague (Czech Republic), Lithic Laboratory University of Leiden (the Netherlands) and Institute of Archaeology ASCR Brno, Research Center for Paleolithic and Paleoethnology Dolní Věstonice.

The project was started with the aim to apply combined techniques of use-wear analysis, initiated by R. Tringham (the "low-power" method) and by L. Keeley (the "high-power" method) during the mid-1970s, employing the improved methodology used in the Lithic Laboratory at the University of Leiden, to stone assemblages of Pavlov, an important upper Palaeolithic site in the Czech Republic. The research was purposely turned to a verification of the possibility to employ use-wear analysis as a routine part of upper Palaeolithic, especially Gravettian, excavations. At the beginning of the project, very few micro-wear Palaeolithic researches had been published and those analyses were made mostly on Magdalenian assemblages as the older periods were supposed to be rather unsuitable for micro-wear analysis. This situation changed radically during the last three years as it was obvious at the Use-wear conference held in Verona 2005 where a lot of traceologists presented their researches done on Palaeolithic tools and the results presented there corresponded mostly with my findings and approved the employment of the method for the (at least upper) Palaeolithic.

A lithic use-wear experimentation, a necessary part of the microwear research, was performed but not so extensively (in comparison with the others; Vaughan N=249, Gijn N=310, etc.) as this was not the object of the research and I had a possibility to compare the researched material with the experimental tools collection made in Leiden (over 500 pieces). In addition, the analysed Palaeolithic assemblages consisted of previously experimentally researched and published raw materials, i.e. the experimental approach to formation of use-wear traces on cryptocrystalline silicates (flint, chert and radiolarite) was not a main part of this research. However, the basic experimental program was designed to test possible contact materials and common usages of stone tools expected in prehistoric periods.

During the research program more upper Palaeolithic sites were included: a Gravettian assemblage (about 25-28 000 BP) from the site Pavlov and Dolní Věstonice, a late Upper Palaeolithic assemblage from karstic areas (late Palaeolithic, Magdalenian, Mesolithic) and Bohunician/Aurignacian assemblages (about 33 - 40 000 PB) from Stránská skála. Besides the functional composition of the excavated stone-tool assemblages, the study focused on the relations between the discernible function, the typology and the length of the settlements.

Because in many cases the sites and their stone-tool inventories were huge, it was impossible to analyse all chipped-stone material which had been excavated. That is why only representative samples were chosen. It is expected that the study presented here will be an impulse to other anthropologists and archaeologists to employ use-wear analyses in their researches as the data provided could be an important piece of the ancient life mosaic despite the fact that the analysis is still a rare exception in the Czech Republic.

1. Introduction to the method and history of use-wear analysis

Use-wear analysis (or also called traceology or microwear analysis) is a microscopic method that tries to interpret use-wear traces appearing on a tool surface during its usage. This scientific method was originally developed as an auxiliary method in criminalistics. Its application to prehistoric artefacts was established during the 1970s.

The desire to reconstruct the usage of stone tools in ancient or prehistoric times dates to the early days of the Prehistoric Archaeology. As far back as history dates, the archaeologists have been struggling with the problem of the functional interpretation of the unknown found artefacts as not always it is possible to estimate the function upon the analogies with ethnographic descriptions based on contemporary native societies. The majority of prehistoric populations lived in conditions and ecosystems which we are not able to fully reconstruct. Also, a lot of activities have been completely lost during thousands of years of the human history. Thus, it could be even more difficult to go much further to the history and imagine the life of early hominids having only the knowledge of an everyday behaviour in the contemporary native societies. At the moment, the archaeologists rely on mere hypothesis. Therefore, the effort was put on developing a method providing reliable additional information about the found artefacts and their usage.

The classic typological method of assigning "functional" names and qualities to prehistoric stone tools was usually based on ethnological or historical analogies and on a similarity of a tool shape. Throughout the 19th century and even up until the 1960s pre-historians followed various ways to achieve reliable functional interpretations of a growing body of the lithic material. These efforts coincided with the need to set the great mass of the tool data into coherent chronological and geographical classifications. However, the first attempts were quite unsystematic, related only to the respective archaeological research.

In the 1950s a Russian archaeologist S. Semenov was the first one, who started with the systematic experimental approach and regularly employed a microscope, inspired by the criminalistic method. Once his work "Pervobytnaja technika" (1957) was published in English in 1964, explosion of use-wear researches has been initiated in the Western Europe and USA.

Even prior to Semenov's influence in lithic studies, there were a number of archaeologists who were aware of the significance of wear traces for the proper functional interpretation. Not at all uncommon were reports of simple visual examination of the heavily developed traces caused by the tool usage. The main phenomena (edge rounding, striations, lustrous polish) observed on tools were associated with the working activities (e.g. Spurrell 1892; Evans 1872). During the nineteenth and the first half of the twentieth centuries a large number of experiments were conducted on stone tools in order to test the capability of a given tool type in accomplishing the function(s) which had been attributed to it over the years. Although such "efficiency studies" were instrumental in indicating certain functional possibilities of the tested stone implements, the formation of use-wear patterns was generally not studied at the same time. Another type of tool-use experimentation at the time consisted of "direct verification" (Keeley 1974), in which the researcher conducts only such tests as are thought necessary to support or disprove a given functional hypothesis for a certain class of implements, with the major emphasis being placed on comparison of experimental and prehistoric use-wear patterns (e.g. Spurrell 1892; Curwen 1930; Bruijn 1958/59). Still, tool-use experimentation and the observation of wear traces were for the most part non-systematic and of limited scope and scientific control. Furthermore, examination of the use-wear remained essentially macroscopic, since a microscope was rarely applied due to problems of functional interpretation. However, these tool-using experiments constituted an important first attempt to break away from the speculative approach, based solely on analogy and "conventional wisdom" (e.g. Sonnenfield 1964). The direct observations of prehistoric edge wear attributes combined with practical attempts to recreate these in detail meant that the study of the function of ancient flint tools began to change into an archaeological discipline, with its own independent data set. The amount of wear was related to the length of work, but also to the grain-size of the raw material.

Semenov's significant basic contribution was to demonstrate the necessity of systematic tool-use experimentation and microscopic examination of wear-traces. Semenov took into account all the traces of wear which result from manufacture, use and natural agencies - polishes, striations, rounding, cracks, edge scarring. His traceological manual gave primary consideration to striation, in accord with his emphasis on reconstructing the "kinematics" (motions) of a stone-tool use (Semenov 1957, 1968). But since Semenov's publications and those of his associates at the Leningrad Academy of Science were only rarely available in English or French, very little was known about the actual procedures of their traceological method or about precise details of their experimental and archaeological analyses since 1947. The lack of available details caused serious problems for analysts who tried to apply Semenov's method to either experimental tools, ethnographic material (e.g. Gould et al. 1971) or to prehistoric collections. Disappointment and disillusionment followed as one investigator after another found Semenov's results impossible to substantiate (Keeley and Newcomer 1977).

The fundamental rules of regarding the interpretation of use-wear traces were postulated during this first stage of use-wear researches. Since striations were not found to form on flint tools as often as it would be expected from Semenov's book, some researchers decided to turn to other types of use-wear for functional identification: edge chipping (Tringham et al. 1974; Odell 1975; Odell and Odell-Vereecken 1980; Shea 1988), polishes (Keeley 1980; Keeley and Newcomer 1977) and non-organic residues (Anderson 1980; Anderson-Gerfaud 1981). Accordingly, L. Keeley, H. Tringham and G. H. Odell are considered the founders of the method, beside Semenov. The early researches in 1970s were characteristic by their great expectations and enthusiasm about the possibility that the methods would be able to provide the exact identification of worked materials (e.g. to differentiate between tree and herbal species). Also it was in this period when two different methodological approaches of the interpretation of use-wear traces were formulated - Low Power Approach (LPA), using a binocular/stereoscopic microscope with a magnification up to 100x; and High Power Approach (HPA), using an incident light microscope with a magnification at least 100-300x.

The use-wear traces form on the surface of a tool, at the contact with the worked material. The observed traces can be divided into 2 groups. The first group includes traces connected with the edge removals (edge rounding and scarring, so called "use retouch") visible with a low magnification and therefore preferably used for LPA interpretation. R. Tringham and several of her students published the results of the first wide-ranging series of microwear tests (Tringham et al. 1974). The experiments controlled for the variables of a lithic raw material, worked material, use motion, non-use damage, number of strokes, mode of prehension, intentional retouch, pressure and the contact angle. The experimental flint edges were examined under a stereoscopic microscope and as the most useful they ascertained magnification of 40-60x (Tringham et al. 1974). Edge damage in the form of microchipping or microscarring was the principal wear phenomenon recorded, according to the attributes of the distribution, size, shape and sharpness of the edge of the microflake scars. Tringham et al. (1974) concluded that there was sufficient patterning in the experimental edge-scarring results to warrant functional analyses of prehistoric stone-tool assemblages on the basis of microflaking attributes. Specifically, the prehistoric use motion (longitudinal, transverse, rotative) and the relative degree of hardness of the contact material (hard, medium, soft) could be interpreted from microscar patterns.

Functional analysis by low-power microscopic inspection of edge scarring involves uncomplicated equipment (a stereoscopic microscope) and can proceed at a relatively rapid time once the analyst is experienced (Tringham et al. 1974). Although G. Odell has been most instrumental in further refining of the "low-power" method (Odell 1977, 1981), in development of a descriptive system for edge removals and undertaking additional use-wear experimentation with the method (Odell 1980; Odell and Odell-Vereecken 1980), the edge removals were also included in "Keeley's high-power approach" (see below) from the start (Keeley 1980).

Many of the papers presented at the first symposium on microwear topics (the Conference on Lithic; Use-Wear, Vancouver, Canada, March 1977) dealt with various experimental aspects of the microflaking approach and the physical principles behind edge chipping on stone tools (Hayden 1979). The main problem with inferring a tool function from edge removals is that there are various ways in which they can occur. First, micro-chipping results as a by-product of intentional retouching, for example of a scraper edge (Brink 1978a; Plew and Woods 1985). Such micro-chipping is almost indistinguishable from edge damage due to intentional use (Vaughan 1985a). Secondly, edge damage can result from non-intentional factors during or after the time of inhabitation, such as trampling, transport and soil compaction (Flenniken and Haggerty 1979; Vaughan 1985a) In addition, micro-chipping can occur when the tool is excavated, sieved, transported in bulk, or scattered onto table and rebagged (Gijn 1990). Furthermore, not all types of use result in edge scarring and rounding.

The second group of use wear traces involves the use-wear polish (micropolish) and striations. Some can be observed with a naked eye, while others are only visible at high magnifications in the optical microscope or in the scanning electron microscope (SEM). Striations are grooves and scratches of varying dimension, which are thought to be caused by abrasive particles or grit. They can be a result of intentional work or the natural phenomena. Micropolish is modification of the original tool surface topography and reflectivity as a result of contact with other materials. This change can appear after a few minutes of work at the very edge of the used tool. The polish first develops on the elevated parts of the surface microrelief and then it can eventually spread into the lower areas as the work proceeds. The general progression of polish formation is dependent on the length and intensity of the work, the character of contact substance and movement of the tool in that substance, but also on the raw material the tool was made from. Micropolish formation and morphology are to some extend specific for different kinds of worked materials and constitute the backbone of HPA interpretation.

Similarly to Tringham, Keeley conducted a wide range of use-wear experiments to test the variables of the lithic material, worked material, action, use duration, edge angle, contact angle and intentional retouch (Keeley and Newcomer 1977; Keeley 1980). Keeley employed a compound microscope to view primarily micropolishes and striations at magnifications of up to 400x, but microphotography and interpretation were routinely carried out at 200x. Keeley's "high-power" approach to microwear analysis has concentrated on distinguishing among general categories of worked materials on the basis of the reflectivity, surface texture, topographical features and distribution of the polishes which the contact materials produce on used flint edges. Consecutive high-power microwear experimentation has been conducted, for example, by P. Anderson-Gerfaud (1981), M. E. Mansur-Franchomme (1983), E. Moss (1983a, 1983b, 1986), H. Plisson (1982), Vaughan (1985a), Knutsson (1988a) and many others. There has been an overall high degree of replicability and agreement reported for the micropolishes resulting from these various experimental projects.

Interest in the polishes has stemmed from the demonstration that micropolishes are able to provide information about the category, not just the hardness of a material worked with a flint implement - i.e. stone, bone, antler, wood, hide and plant. Consistent patterns of micropolishes obtained in repeated independent tests have established the usefulness of the high-power approach in determining the modes of utilisation of archaeological flint assemblages. It has been pointed out that such degree of precision is gained at the expense of costlier equipment and a slower speed of analysis than using the low-power microchipping method, which can determine only the relative hardness of the worked material (Odell and Odell-Vereecken 1980).

The Odells have formulated four hardness categories:

- soft materials (meat, skin, leaves): the size of the scars is small with a feather terminations
- soft medium materials (soft woods): large scarring, usually with feather terminations
- hard medium materials (hard woods, soaked antler, fresh bones): hinged scarring of medium-to-large size
- hard materials (bone, antler): typified by stepped terminations of medium-to-large size

However, other experiments asserted the problem with the interpretation of tool function just on the basis of micro-scarring as there is far more variability in flake-scar morphology, location and distribution than was initially claimed by the early proponents of the low-power approach. Tringham et al. (1974) stated that a longitudinal motion produces bifacial, discontinuous scarring, while transverse motions correlate with unifacial, continuous scarring. Vaughan (1985a) carried on an extensive experimental programme and arrived at a different conclusion: while bifacial scarring predominated on tools used in a longitudinal motion (65%), it was by no means absent on edges used for a transverse motion. Even more surprising was Vaughan's conclusion that 52% of the tools used in a transverse motion exhibited no continuous scarring at all. Further, Vaughan's experiments indicated that there is a wide range of scar sizes resulting from each hardness category, whereas termination also does not always correspond with the Odells' scale or the micro chipping is often absent despite intensive usage (Vaughan 1985a). In Vaughan's experiments this phenomenon was noted for 16% of tools used in transverse motions and 18% for those employed in longitudinal motions. As to worked materials, 39% of the edges involving soft contact materials and 6% of those relating to hard materials sustained no microscarring whatsoever (cf. Den Dries and Gijn 1997).

The boom and the optimistic phase of traceology in 1970s stopped in the middle of 80s, when doubts about the method objectivity appeared, together with the other old interpretations, in general accepted at Palaeolithic archaeology at that time. During this introspective/self-critical phase a number of critical articles appeared and disappointment and scepticism prevailed (Juel Jensen 1988). Researches and the methodological approaches were deeply cross-examined by blind tests on the international level to test not only the individual microwear analysts, but to check the method itself (Newcomer et al. 1986; Unrath et al. 1986; Moss 1987a). During these tests the results of interpretations of each scientist were checked not only for the experimental pieces but also for the prehistoric tools. The first conclusions of blind tests brought deep scepticism about distinctiveness of not only different species but even kinds of worked materials (mainly for polishes related to wood, bone and antler). It seemed that the appearance of the polishes made by these materials overlapped to a certain extent. This ascertainment has initiated wide methodological researches including numerous series of experiments with different worked materials in different states. In addition, the other variables than the worked materials which can affect the appearance of polishes, e.g. use motion, duration of use, postdepositional effects and laboratory cleaning were underscored by blind tests. Those made some in the archaeological community dismiss the method in its present state (Newcomer et al. 1986). The criticism offered by Newcomer et al. was due partly to a misperception of the nature of HPA as en exact measuring technique (Juel Jensen 1988).

One of the most important developments in microwear research since the introduction of Semenov's work to the West has been the realisation that use-wear experimentation must be conducted in a comprehensive, systematic way. Although Semenov's work was more systematic and more comprehensive than any previous use-wear research, his contribution lies more in the recognition of the many variables which may affect use-wear and in the technical advances in observing and recording traces, than in a systematic application of experimentation to provide unequivocal statements about the influence of variables on use-wear (Seitzer Olausson 1980). However, the functional analysis of a prehistoric assemblage cannot be based on a limited number of use-wear tests used as a direct verification method of analysis. This means that an analyst must perform or have access to the results of a comprehensive framework of use-wear experiments. The starting point for use-wear analysts became understanding the formation of use-wear traces for different materials based on extensive experimental work and after gaining this experience to provide a possible interpretation of found prehistoric use-wear traces, considering the postdepositional modifications of the artefact surface.

The major new trends in microwear were based on wide frameworks of tests designed to control a number of variables which influence the production of wear by use and non-use factors. New researches (Plisson 1986; Plisson and Mauger 1988; Levi-Sala 1986, 1993, 1996) were pointed to replication and/or simulation of the postdepositional modification of the surface of prehistoric artefacts and previously developed use-wear traces (i.e. patina, trampling, impact of soil chemicals and etc.).

Moreover, the resulting microwear attributes - especially microchipping and polishes - have been analysed and published in greater details than was the case with the results of earlier wear studies to provide other scientists with important comparative data. At the same time, the processes behind the formation of wear phenomena have also been investigated. Techniques of observing microwear have advanced considerably. The use of stereoscopic and compound microscopes has become routine and the special capabilities of the scanning electron microscope have been enlisted.

This was unlike the earlier procedure when firstly the traces were found and simply proved by a simple experiment. To avoid errors arising from the convergence of wear patterns of diverse origins, each hypothesis about utilisation should be considered against a framework of experiments and/or ethnographic comparisons, in order to enable the investigator to say that certain implements have been used in a particular manner on a particular material, not merely because direct verification proved positive, but also because many other experiments or ethnographic comparisons have shown that no other use in any other manner or on any other material is capable of producing similar wear patterns (Keeley 1974).

Concurrent with the adoption of a wide range of use-wear tests, there has been an equally important change in functional research. The systematic and detailed microscopic analysis of wear patterns, mainly with respect to attributes of microchipping, polishes and non-organic residues.

The researches were aimed to discover the origin and the development of use-wear polishes; whether it is mainly physical (abrasion mode; see e.g. Diamond 1979; Meeks et al. 1982; Unger-Hamilton 1984; Levi-Sala 1988, 1993; Yamada 1993) or rather chemical process (silica gel model see e.g. Whitthoft 1967; Del Bene 1979; Kamminga 1979; Anderson 1980). It was also questioned how much the worked material contributes to polish development via integration of its particles into the tool surface. These questions have not been sufficiently solved yet, because it seems that polishes are being formed by both factors depending on the kind of the worked material. It is proved that materials with a high content of silica or collagen (for example cereals, reeds and bones) provide extensive polish. Further, the content of water (or rather hydrogen) in the silica structure and in the contact (worked) materials was analysed and the role of water in use-wear polish development was studied (Andersen and Whitlow 1983; Juel Jensen 1994; cf. Levi-Sala 1993).

Patricia Anderson-Gerfaud has demonstrated experimentally that plant and animal mineral residues which replicate cell membrane structure or cell shape could be trapped into a layer of polish (amorphous silica gel) which forms in the working area of a stone edge as a result of the possible dissolution of silica in the tool surface during the contact with the worked material. Since some durable residues (e.g. phytoliths) may retain their shapes and are comparable to the mineral components of the modern samples, these residues could therefore give more precise identifications of the plant and wood types or animal tissues worked by prehistoric tools (e.g. Anderson 1980; Jahren et al. 1997). Further research into structured residues could add greater depth to lithic functional analyses and more specific paleoeconomic and paleoenviromental reconstructions.

The necessity of more detailed examination of the structure of the polish led to employing the capacity of the electron microscope for use-wear analyses. Patricia Anderson-Gerfaud has expanded the polish method by using the scanning electron microscope up to 10 000x magnification to investigate structured non-organic residues which are contained in the micropolishes formed on stone-tool edges used to work plant, arboreal and animal substances (Anderson 1980; Anderson-Gerfaud 1981; Mansur 1983; Mansur-Franchomme 1983; Knutsson 1988a; Evans and Donahue 2005). Previously, the electron microscope had been used by a number of researchers to obtain better resolution of the features on worn tool surfaces than is possible under high magnification with optical microscopes. But although the electron microscope allows for much higher magnification and consequently more detailed image of the tool surface, this application has not brought as much significant improvement in the use-wear interpretation of worked material as it was originally expected (Anderson-Gerfaud 1981). In addition, electron microscope analysis is much more expensive than the conventional usage of incident light microscope method. However, other different types of microscopes with alternative or improved observing features, adjustments and techniques have been tested for microanalysis, e.g. ion beam analysis techniques (Andersen and Whitlow 1983), energy dispersion analysis (Gijn 1990), confocal laser scanning microscope and fluorescent light (Derndarsky and Ocklind 2001), proton induced X-ray emission spectroscopy and Rutherford back scattering (Evans and Donahue 2005), etc.

The new direction in the methodological approach became a research for the objective quantification of observed traits of use-wear traces (Dumont 1982; Grace et al. 1985, 1987, 1996; Beyries et al. 1988; Grace 1989; Yamada and Sawada 1993) and development of automatic expert database systems (FAST, WAWES, TECHAN ...) which would be independently able to interpret the worked material after entering defined features of observed traces, according to data obtained during the experimental works. Unfortunately, this direction has not come up to expectations because the variability of use-wear traces in combination with a different extent of postdepositional modifications allows only for a subjective description and therefore it is too complex and sensitive for an automatic computer decision (e.g. Knutsson 1988b). Moreover, the usage of these artificially designed decision-making systems by different scientists was rather problematic mainly for the difficulties with creating the distinctive categories of the features of the observed traces as a part of the objective descriptive model. However, it is possible that such a model will be developed and decision-making systems will offer easy and correct results in the future. Their development has already contributed to improvements and standardizations of the use-wear methodology. However, the research of possible ways of quantifying the texture or reflectivity of polishes is considered to be fruitless until the nature of polishes is better understood.

Microwear analysis has gone through a historical development similar to the other relatively new disciplines. After the initial elation phase came a phase during which many researchers were confronted with a variety of problems. Since 90s, the method has gradually moved into the next phase, characterized by a more well-balanced use with an awareness of the possibilities and limitations. Moreover, use-wear analysis can help in investigation of interdependencies between techniques and cultural systems by linking two (or more) "artefact" categories to give glimpses of various "chaînes opératoire" and thereby contribute to the subject of "the anthropology of technique" and move the method beyond a purely functional approach of the functional analysis of tools (Gijn 1990; Grace 1996).

1.1 Traceology versus typology

Once prehistoric artefacts are selected for classification as data, the next step is their assignment to a particular typology category. This is a more exact and detailed process that follows from the initial classification and involves not only a general recognition of an artefact as a "tool" but also its measurements and the location of specific modifications on the tool itself. The possible working activity can be deduced from the features of use-wear traces found on the tool's surface. The "tool" in traceology is being understood as an artefact used for any working activity; unlike the "typological insertion" into a system from the view of archaeologists. This incoherency introduces many (sometimes hidden) discrepancies or even contradictions connected with the initial approach of the two independently developed methods, typology and traceology. Therefore, it is necessary to understand their definition of artefacts described as "tools".

In archaeology a typology is the result of the classification of things according to their characteristics.

It is based on a view of the world known from Plato's metaphysics called essentialism. Essentialism is the idea that the world is divided into real, discontinuous and immutable "kinds". This idea forms the basis for most typological constructions, particularly of stone artefacts where essential forms are often thought of as "mental templates", or combinations of traits that are favoured by the maker. Variations in the artefact forms and attributes are seen as a consequence of the imperfect realization of the template and are usually attributed to differences in raw material properties or individuals' technical competences (Hill and Evans 1972).

Typology, as a scientific method, started to be formed in 1891 when A. de Mortillet established a concept of "industry" in archaeology as a specific set of tools accompanying respective prehistoric culture. The first proposals of typological nomenclatures (G. de Mortillet, J. Déchelett, H. Breuil, V. de Pradenne) were rather simple descriptive terminologies based on a subjective definition of attributes which differed from almost each archaeologist and, therefore, artefacts names were mostly incomparable with other archaeologists' descriptions (Fridrich 1997). For this reason since 40-50s of the 20th century the first internationally accepted nomenclatures, common for all scientists, started to be formulated. These first nomenclatures corresponded with the era they were created and reflected the influence of then strongly accepted classic evolutionism according to which all progressive evolutional changes in Palaeolithic industries correspond with the changes of a biological evolution of the humankind and the society.

In the 19th and early 20th century archaeological typologies were usually constructed using a combination of empirical observation and intuition. With the development of statistical techniques and numerical taxonomy in the 1960s, mathematical methods (including Cluster analysis, Principal components analysis, Correspondence analysis and Factor analysis) have been used to build typologies (Dunnell 1986).

During the first half of the 20th century plenty of typological nomenclatures evolved which considered different classifications of possible tool's attributes. Gradually, the three approaches to creating a typological nomenclature have appeared, but only the first one is being widely used for descriptions of Palaeolithic industries nowadays. The first approach was represented by a group of French scientists (F. Bordes, D. de Soneville-Bordes, J. Perrot), who understood the tool type more or less intuitively as a shape which was repeatedly created mainly by a specifically located retouch. The shape has a particular name and reflects specific aspects of human thinking, characteristic for the respective time period. This approach relies on contemporary ethnographic parallels in which the significant artefacts have their own particular names and the nomenclature of different types corresponds with the language structure (Svoboda 1999). Bordes' method allowed for relative comparison of tools of different ages and/or provenance and opened door to further possibilities of a statistic processing of prehistoric industries. Regarding to the extension of his work and permanent validity of his nomenclature, F. Bordes is being understood as a founder of the typology despite the other predecessors. Bordes' method dominated in 50s and 60s of the 20th century and is being used (mainly for Palaeolithic industries) with a few modifications nowadays (cf. Klíma 1956; Fridrich 1997, 2005).

The second approach resulted from the effort to make the rating of a prehistoric industry as much objective as possible via definition of general characteristics which could be processed by computers, using the statistic methods. According to this group of archaeologists (for example G. Laplace, H. de Lumley, T. Weber or D. Maniu) the "type" results from the complex statistic analysis and correlations of the attributes which are in concord. The "type" is understood as a complex of repeatedly appearing attributes (raw material, retouch, production process etc.) This "analytic" typology believes that the above described "descriptive" nomenclature is incorrect and the "type" name is for the higher objectiveness replaced with numbers (Malina 1980). This allows to code the "tool type" as a number system and consequently to compare them via statistic analysis. In case of the use of statistic evaluations the first approach may seem to be more subjective and the second more objective, but the "objectiveness" could be illusory (Svoboda 1999). However, in everyday practical application, the numerical system is barely used, only for some extra analysis or the extension of the classic Bordes' nomenclature to counterpoint specific features of the studied industries with using the numeral indexes (Klíma 1956; Fridrich 2005). As an integrating approach for the Boarder's typology and the statistic comparison could be considered the morphometric analysis (e.g. Fridrich and Sýkorová 2005).

Lewis R. Binford tried to present a third approach to the industry nomenclature. Based on ethnographic comparisons, he claimed that tool typology not necessarily has always some ethnic or social meaning (Svoboda 1999). From his view, the "tool type" is not the cultural indication, but it should more reflect the real tool function which it was intended to be used for. Binford's nomenclature points to all stages of the tool production (human behaviour and activities connected with the tool production) more then to the very result of the production, the tool itself. The analysis should include not only the retouched pieces but all the debris which arose while the tool was made. Binford's intention was to describe the integration of the artefact into the complex system and point mainly to the function of the tool (Binford 1982). Typology, in his conception, tries to determine the relations between the specific forms of cultures, different environments and economy, where every single element can have a different role/function in each system. L Binford did not create a "new" nomenclature in the very sense of the word, but he rather extended the understanding of the "tool" in the context of everyday activities of the prehistoric society.

As it is evident from the above described approaches to understanding of the "tool type" and creating of unified nomenclature, there is a serious contradiction between the function and the form already in the typology itself. Further, each of these approaches has its advantages and disadvantages. On the contrary, traceology focuses more or less only in the tool function. Necessarily, in some cases, the conflict between the typological classification (tool name) and the real way of its use (function) must appear. This means that the tool "scraper" would not have been necessarily used for "scraping" but for example for cutting or other different working activity. Also there is not always obvious a clear relation between the retouch distribution and the specific type or location of the use-wear traces.

Several comparative studies on functional analysis have indicated that no single tool type can be confidently assigned to either a single manner of use or worked material on a scale greater than that of the individual site. However, it is possible within different sites to observe correlations between metrical/morphological attributes of particular tool types and various functions (e.g. tool thickness, the edge curvature and etc. specific to worked material or activity). This would suggest that, if one is interested in function, it is generally more appropriate to look at the characteristic of the individual edges, than the overall shape of tool, as was also stressed in ethnoarchaeological studies (e.g. Gould et al. 1971; White et al. 1977; Hayden 1979). It is also clear that the retouched edges of the formal tool types need not to be the only utilised part of the tool's perimeter. Furthermore, many of the studies have demonstrated that many unretouched artefacts, in typological terms waste products or not tools, have in fact been utilised and can considerably contribute to better understanding of the daily activities carried out at the various sites.

However, every artefact is changing dynamically during the time of its use, having its own specific history and, in the course of time, can change its shape and/or function. This is most typical for Middle Palaeolithic scrapers (Dibble 1995) or ancient Egyptian knives (Svoboda 1999), which were continuously used and re-sharpened. The function could be changed when the tool was damaged or broken and then "repaired" or "remade" into a different tool type. Nevertheless, the previous use-wear traces can remain on the surface of such a remade tool and may be in an illusory contradiction to its new function.

The micro-wear analyses demonstrate that the method is not only capable of producing interesting though trivial functional interpretations of individual artefacts, but also that traceology can provide more general statements to study of tool using and tool manufacturing behaviour (Keeley 1981; Plisson 1982; Jensen 1982; Gendel 1982; Dumont 1983; Moss 1983a). Such information offers prehistorians the opportunity to check the validity of imposed "functional types" and to differentiate attributes of tool morphology relating to function from those of apparently non-functional or stylistic significance (Dumont 1987).

Although, it would be fallacious to automatically associate a certain tool type with a specific function, this does not imply that typology have become worthless. It is still necessary and very valuable for classification of assemblages but it also has a great use as a temporal or spatial marker (cf. Tomášková 2003).

1.2 Interpretative possibilities and limits of the method

Microwear analysis can be a tool for solving questions regarding the form and function of implements and the activities and tasks carried out by the inhabitants of a settlement. At an intra-site level, functional data can assist in the search for activity areas. Traceology is an interpretational procedure and, as in most archaeology, some materials carry more information than do others. Thus, the level of resolution is better for some categories of wear traces than for others and that inference on function must respect these conditions.

Most of working activities leave a visible record at the surface of a tool in a form of specific modification. The use-wear traces can be visible just by a naked eye but for a more detailed interpretation, the microscopic analysis must be performed. Recent studies were also focused on a "positive" form of a use interpretation. When the tool is examined immediately after it was uncovered from the layer and the surface is kept intact, it is sometimes possible to find also the organic residues of the worked materials and interpret the tool function with the

knowledge of the exact type of worked material (e.g. Hardy et al. 2001)

The interpretation of the microwear traces requires a systematic methodological approach taking into account variations in rocks, materials worked and morphologies of the tools, as well as the relative ecological and cultural situation of the sites, and last but not least the natural agencies effecting the surface of prehistoric chipped tools. The terms "interpretation" and "identification" play a key role in traceological methodology. The identification means the definite determination of the exact function, worked material etc. which is supported by the historical records or other direct evidence and therefore it is for 100% sure that the determination is correct. On the other hand, the "interpretation" involves, to a certain extent, a subjective explanation of found evidence (use-wear traces) which is interpreted upon the scientist's previous experience and opinion. The interpretation can correspond with the prehistoric reality but not necessarily. The rate of objectiveness of any interpretation can be evaluated by the concordance with other analysts and proven via blind tests on experimental pieces.

The possibilities of the micro-wear method are to a great extent limited by the following factors:

- raw material from which the tool was chipped and its coarseness
- contact material which was worked by the tool
- time and intensity of using the tool
- total age of the tool
- postdepositional modifications affecting the tool surface not only during its deposition in soil matrix but also during its excavation and examination and as well its following storage in depository

The use quality of the tool is determined also by the quality and homogeneity of the raw material used for tool chipping, i.e. whether its structure is compact like for example with obsidian and cryptocrystalline silicates (flint, chert, radiolarite) or whether it consists of small grains or crystals like quartz or quartzite. The character of the raw material influences not only the chipping options of a tool (the length and angle of the edge), but later it also affects the development of the use-wear traces. Especially, the non-homogeneous raw materials may be quite specific from the use-wear point of view, as the releasing of the grains from the edge during the contact with a worked material on one hand can improve the edge quality due to "self-sharpening", but on the other hand the edge removal of the very edge can be faster than the development of the use-wear traces. In general, the coarser the raw material is, the slower is the formation of the polish and striations. Normally, polish develops topographically, so that the surface ridges and elevation are the first to change, forming circumscribed spots of polish components. These are broken or surrounded by the dark, unchanged, low-lying areas. As work proceeds the lower areas slowly become polished too, so that the individual polish components are gradually linked. The ultimate end product is an unbroken polished surface. The reason, why larger percentage of coarse-grained tools is interpreted as being "unused" than of fine-grained specimens, is that the polish is developed on the highest points of the surface and it takes it longer to join into the visible spots of polish. The initial stage of polish formation during which no characteristic attributes are yet developed (i.e. the visible distinctive spots have not been formed) prevails much longer and can be overlooked or hidden.

Likewise, the hardness of raw material contributes to the level of development of the use-wear traces because for harder raw materials it may take significantly longer before the use-wear traces are developed then for the softer ones. For this reason, the development of the use-wear traces is understood only as a relative indicator and it is not possible to make a general quantification neither in time nor intensity units (i.e. it is not possible to estimate the exact worked time in hours/minutes, etc.). In addition, the type of the raw material can influence the persistence of use-wear polishes during the tool deposition in soil matrix. The experiments with chemical alternation of micropolishes demonstrated that, for example, all polishes on the Tertiary flint were destroyed more quickly than those on the Cretaceous flint (Plisson and Mauger 1988). In general, the lower is the degree of recrystallization of silica the less is the raw material resistant to chemical attack.

No mater which raw material it was made from, every used tool may display two kinds of use-wear traces: the edge removals and/or polishes. Degree of their development depends on the hardness of a contact (worked) material, the time/intensity of working activity and the following postdepositional forces.

The edge removals, sometimes also called "use-retouch", develop as the effect of edge stabilization during the tool use and correspond with the hardness of contact material and the direction of a tool movement. The principle of "use-retouch" origin is pretty similar to the manufacturing of the "intentional retouch" (made to change the tool shape and edges via microchipping) and which, as I supposed, might have been probably inspired by the "use-retouch". The difference in appearance of the "use-retouch" and "intentional retouch" is more or less made by a systematic approach during the intentional retouching when the microchipping is made usually on one side of the edge. Also, the "intentional retouch" is to a certain extent standardized in the size and shape of microflakes. Moreover, there is a high regularity and a functional intention in its distribution on the tool edges. The "intentional retouch" supports the edge stabilization and prevents the extensive edge removals which usually appear during the very first moments of a tool usage (mainly when hard contact materials are worked). For this reason, if the intentional retouch is present on the analysed edge, the interpretation possibilities, based solely on the edge removals (LPA) without further analysis of polishes, are significantly miner because the development of edge removals was influenced, limited and/or masked by the intentional retouch. The special type of the edge removal is the edge rounding.

Obviously, the degree of edge damages corresponds with the tool shape, whether the tool selected for the task had the most suitable working edges. Moss (1983b) demonstrated that edges with a straight cross-section are much more efficient for various tasks and do not get damaged so quickly as irregular edges (see also Kaminga 1982). This relate to Plew and Wood's (1985) observations, that tools which worked efficiently sustained far less edge damage than those which were obviously inappropriate for the activity. This is necessary to bear in mind during the comparison of the experimental results with the prehistoric tools as their users were much more aware of stone tools nature and its convenience for a respective activity. Therefore, the edge damage could be more frequent on experimental than on prehistoric tools.

According to edge damage attributes, the worked material hardness can be approximately estimated. But some used materials might be available in several hardness categories, moreover they can continually overpass from one state to another. Generally, the worked material can be divided into two or more hardness categories, but the exact distinctive line between the categories cannot be set (see the previous chapter).

The use-wear polishes are specific modification of the tool surface at the place of a contact with the worked material. The exact mechanism of its development has not been found and it seems that it can be different for different groups of contact materials. The interpretation of contact materials based on polishes allows for interpreting of the group of contact materials in categories: wood, hide, bone, antler, cereals etc. However, the ability to distinguish between the contact materials is not given by different kinds of polishes, specific for every contact material, but due to the different attributes of a developed polish (e.g. the extension, distribution, localisation, topography, etc.) and the other features that appear in the polish structure. The contact material must be interpreted according to a combination of all attributes because any attribute itself is not unique for the respective contact material and only their specific combination makes the polish view "characteristic" for the respective contact material. Therefore, in some cases it can be difficult to interpret the contact material as the attributes are sometimes not clear enough to distinguish the groups of close contact materials, especially antler-wood-bone group, as the polish characteristics may overlap. The researches indicate that under certain circumstances it is possible to distinguish among the tree materials (antler-ivory-bone) use wear polishes, but solely on the experimental level (Keeley 1980; Vaughan 1985a). Likewise, the polishes caused by the working of soaked antler and green wood in transverse motion, such as scraping, can be virtually indistinguishable from each other in the early stages of formation, while in a more developed stage they begin to look dissimilar (Keeley 1980; Vaughan 1985a). Therefore, on the basis of what it is known about relevant causes for polish formation and given the fact that published and unpublished blind tests constantly show identification problems (Unrath et al. 1986), most analysts now limit their determination to certain groups of materials, rather then to a specific substance (contact material). The problem is not that the polishes look alike at certain stages, the issue is to be aware of this situation. The group inferences are based on the estimation of the limits of the method and of the foundation on which the conclusion rests. The problem may arise when the interpretation is pushed too far (Juel Jensen 1988).

Polish must develop to a certain stage before it begins to exhibit diagnostic or material-specific features and some wear traces pass that threshold more slowly than others. Subtle materials such as soft vegetable, fat or meat usually do not develop beyond the "generic weak stage" (Vaughan 1985a) or "greasy lustre" (Gijn 1990) even after 60 to 90 min of use. A well developed polish can display different degrees of brightness or reflectivity depending on the texture of the polish surface. Surface topography and relative brightness are the most important polish attributes. Together with the density of polish and the polish extension away from the edge, they constitute some of the main criteria for determining contact material. However, in spite of the growing understanding of formation processes provided by high-technology measuring techniques, micropolish is first and foremost a visual phenomenon. For that reason the HPA is based principally on a formal analogy, comparison of prehistoric wear attributes with experimentally induced ones, without full knowledge of the relationships between these attributes (Juel Jensen 1988).

As the unique feature for a distinction of each specific material does not exist, it is much more precise to speak about an "interpretation" of the worked (contact) material rather then "identification", as we can never be 100% sure about the relation of the observed use-wear traces to the worked prehistoric material and activity. Moreover, some working activities could have involved procedures which had been already forgotten/lost (for example some special additives for the hide processing, etc.) and therefore the use-wear traced provided by the experimental work cannot be fully identical with those found on the prehistoric tools, even leaving aside the postdepositional modifications.

Beside the worked material, use-wear analysis can provide information about kinematics of the used tool edge towards the worked material and, therefore, the probable working activity can be estimated. The description of a direction of the motion is related to the used edge. According to the basic directions of a tool movement during its usage preserved in use-wear traces, the more complex activities can be suggested. Traces with a longitudinal orientation correspond with cutting or sawing. The transversally oriented traces can represent scraping, adzing/wedging, chiselling or planning, depending on the tool type. The traces of a diagonal motion can point to such activities as engraving, chopping, shaving or whittling. The specific traces can be preserved for boring, drilling or piercing.

A special category is represented by the use-wear traces originated from hafting. The traces are connected with the material the haft was made from and the used banding and therefore they can be rather confusing, more so, when the direction of the motion characteristics and location of the use-wear traces on the tool surface are considered. Unfortunately, it seems that the hafting traces are rarely preserved or that it is difficult to uncover and properly interpret them. Especially on Palaeolithic tools, the evidence of hafting is more often indirect and the idea if/how some types of tools were hafted is still rather unclear as the hafts have been found only exceptionally.

The interpretation of the use-wear traces could be methodologically difficult, mainly of Palaeolithic implements, as they are in most cases extensively affected by postdepositional processes that may hide or partially remove the use-wear traces from the tool surface. Considering this restraint, it is necessary to express the degree of analyst's certainty of the use-wear traces interpretation, for example by using the category "unsure". The common use-wear traces reached by working organic materials tend to disappear or loose visibility due to impact of chemicals, either acids or hydroxides. These chemicals are present in the environment and affect the prehistoric artefact for a long time, while it is being deposited in the soil matrix. It seems very probably that the soil chemical composition plays a dominant role in the process of a patina formation and therefore it is logical that the growing age of artefact correlates with a lower probability of the use-wear traces persistence on its surface. In cases where the polish was only weakly developed (either due to a soft worked material or short time of usage), it may be completely removed from the surface of the artefact after a long time affect of chemicals in the soil. Moreover, patina itself decreases the polish brightness and the visibility of the polish structure so the less developed polishes can be almost invisible or not interpretable on such an affected surface. This is probably the reason why the use-wear traces are so rarely preserved on tools from the old Palaeolithic and use-wear analysis is based mainly on LPA, in case that it is performed at all.

However, even if all conditions seem favourable (a minimum of postdepositional modifications, fine-grained raw material) some activities, especially those involving working of meat without tendons and bone or fresh soft green plants or very short time uses in general, can be underrepresented in relation to the polishes caused by harder matters or the working of hides, or the traces might be even completely missing in the analysed assemblage. Obviously, the negative evidence cannot be considered a proof; all other possible found artefacts not only lithic must be considered.

The other problem arising during a functional interpretation of activities and tasks is their location at the site. It is necessary to bear in mind that the location where the tool was found not necessary represents the place where the activity was performed. This can be tricky especially for implements with the evidence of hafting, as the manufacture of hafts was probably a time consuming task, the worn-out implements were brought "home" where the new implements were inserted into hafts. Then, the worn-out flints were discarded far away from the location of their actual use, in hearth areas of the settlement. Thus, a concentration of hide-working implements does not necessarily indicate a hide preparation locus; it might as well be an effect of rehafting or retooling enterprises or secondary disposal procedures (Keeley 1982). And vice versa, some types of used artefacts may have been dislocated from the site whenever the tools were transported from settlement to their location of actual use, i.e. used outside the settlement area. Therefore, the mobility of the tools must be taken into account prior to making any statements about configurations being activity areas.

The last problem deals with the palimpsest of occupations. It is almost impossible to separate various use-instances of a site without contextual evidence (other artefact categories relationship of which can be demonstrated). Use-wear analysis offers a possibility to examine a "real" relation between the artefacts found in the same vertical position (layer), e.g. bones and tools. On the other hand, the numerical specifications of the amount of e.g. wood-working or hide-working implements observed in a given assemblage may reflects just an absurd average of several independent occupation episodes. Therefore, while the microwear analysis can provide important additional information about individual flint objects, this evidence must still be evaluated and assessed in the light of site formation processes and problems (Juel Jensen 1988).

In conclusion, the microwear analysis can add more details to our picture of daily life at the sites, part of which could not have been attained by any other way, but their interpretation must be made responsibly. Microwear analysis cannot be taken as the exact "measuring" technique, i.e. the method does not provide quick and secure answers to whatever question asked concerning the use of specific artefacts, but it is an approach founded on interpretation analogy and based on observations of the clusters of wear attributes that are considered to be relevant to functional inference.

2. Material and Methods

The Palaeolithic material is often supposed to be unsuitable for use-wear analysis due to loss of preservation or high postdepositional modification (Keeley 1980; Anderson-Gerfaud 1981). Nevertheless, other studies have shown that micro-wear traces caused by use could be preserved on even the most ancient African tools (Keeley and Toth 1981) or Middle Palaeolithic tools (Roebroeks et al. 1997). According to these results, use-wear analysis has been attempted on the Moravian Palaeolithic chipped artefacts to prove or disprove the possible source of scientific knowledge.

The main objectives for use-wear analysis were:

- to identify the method of use and the worked material by selected tools and then compare the results with the presumption (anticipation) of archaeologists and other findings from the excavated site,
- to compare sites Stránská skála, Pavlov I, Dolní Věstonice and Karst according to interpreted traces and the length of settlement,
- to compare the typological groups with the determined functional results,
- to test if the selection of the raw material was influenced by a specific function of the tool,
- to compare the functional results of the typological groups with other published analyses,
- to evaluate the potential of both methods of use wear analysis for the analysed Palaeolithic sites.

Interpretation of the contact materials was based on the structure of polishes, striations (HPA) and edge damages (LPA) and compared with the use-wear traces on the experimental tools. The reliability of the method and my capability of the interpretation of observed use-wear traces were repeatedly approved by blind tests performed in Leiden Laboratory, using their extensive collection of experimental tools.

The result part is divided into five chapters: the results for the four analysed sites and the discussion of the most important and frequent types of the chipped tools. The sites results are first discussed per the respective site and the outcomes, when possible, are compared cross-sites. As the sampling of the analysed assemblages differs, only some results are comparable. However, the outputs are structured in the same manner for easier orientation. Discussion of the possible relations between morphology and function was made across all analysed sites and compared with other published use-wear results gained for different cultures and time periods.

2.1 Artefacts

Four different excavations were selected for the analysis: Stránská skála III/IIIa, Pavlov I, Dolní Věstonice II 1999 and selected karstic settlements. Each site represents a slightly different type of settlement and culture. All analysed artefacts came from excavations made by Institute of Archaeology ASCR Brno, where the artefacts are also deposited. Every excavation was then published in a detailed report of wider international project or in series of institutional monographs. As the respective researches were a part of multidisciplinary projects, the sampling was specific to the needs of the research and based on recommendations and requests of the archaeologists.

Usually, controlled site-specific studies include the functional analysis of total or at least well-represented artefact populations at various levels of resolution: a) small assemblages, b) implements associated with a feature at a given site and c) tools and knapping debris

from one or several refitted cores (cf. Juel Jensen and Petersen 1985; Vaughan 1985a; Symens 1986). A second line of sampling can be constituted by thematic studies that focus on particular types of objects, defined by their morphology or technology or by some macroscopically visible use-wear attributes such as the so-called sickle gloss (cf. Meeks et al. 1982; Moss 1983a; Fisher et al. 1984; Unger-Hamilton 1985; Juel Jensen 1986; Anderson-Gerfaud 1986, etc.)

The analysis of the entire collections was usually precluded due to a high number of excavated artefacts, therefore the sampling was based mostly on a) or b) strategy for site studies in a combination with thematic study approach to selected typology groups. The number of pieces which can be examined per day is approximately 5-8 (including the unused pieces). That makes use-wear analysis rather time consuming. The total number of the analysed artefacts was 551 and their typological distribution was as follows in Tab.2-1. For further comparison, tools were divided into more general typological groups. The detailed information about the lithic material and selective criteria for each site are described in the respective chapters.

All analysed pieces were drawn on data sheets with the indication of the exact location of observed wear traces and photos, if they were made to document typical and/or unusual examples of the use and not-use wear traces.

Tab. 2-1 The overview of analysed tools by type and sites distribution.

Typology groups	Typology	Stránská skála	Dolní Věstonice	Pavlov	Karst	Total
Blades	backed blade		2	3	1	6
	blade		19	177	4	200
	crested blade		1	4		5
	retouched blade		1	15	1	17
	truncated blade	2				2
Burins	burin		1	64	1	66
	burin on broken blade			1		1
Combi	burin + notch			2		2
	burin + point			1		1
	endscraper + burin			9		9
Flakes	flake		14	26	9	49
	retouched flake			4		4
Chisels	chisel			7		7
Microliths	backed microblade		2	22		24
	crescent			1		1
	microblade		1	22	5	28
	microcrescent			3	1	4
Others	bec	1		1		2
	borer			2		2
	burin spall			6	1	7
	core				1	1
	core flake			1		1
	chip			2		2
	notch	9		4		13
	pointed bec			1		1
Points	base of point			2		2
	point	1		3		4
	retouched point			1		1
	Font Yves point			1		1
	Levallois point	9				9
Scrapers	endscraper	13		56		69
	scraper			1		1
	sidescraper	7		2		9
Total		42	41	444	24	551

2.2 Experiments

Experimentation constitutes the microwear analysis only frame of reference and it is a necessary step toward development and refinement of inferences about tool functions. Experimental work does not serve just to create a comparative use-wear collection but together with blind tests, experiments also function as a control of the interpretational power of the method and for testing of the sources of errors. In this study, the experimental phase was continuously carried out but was not the main part of the research. However, about 50 experimental tools were used in order to understand the use-wear traces formation and development, as well as to create a small comparative collection of tools. The experimental research focused on materials assumed to be common in a prehistoric life, primarily organic materials such antler, bone, wood, plants, hide and meat but also inorganic materials (soil and ochre). The prehistoric tools were compared with the traces on the experimental tools, using also the extensive collection of experimental tools (over 1000 pieces) in Leiden Laboratory. The Leiden collection was mostly used for my study and apprehension of the use-wear traces at all.

2.3 Technical equipment

It used to be emphasized that comparability between various use-wear studies can be only achieved when similar equipment is employed (Moss 1983a, 1986; Gijn 1990). But the technical values of clarity, sharpness and depth of field provided by the leading companies Olympus and Nikon have developed to a very similar level during the last years, so that the data obtained on these microscopes are easily comparable.

Every tool was analysed in two ways - implementing both approaches: LPA using a binocular microscope with up to 100x magnification or by using a hand lens, and HPA using the light incident microscope with up to 300x magnification (Olympus BXFM). This type of the microscope allows a sectional adjustment of its elements composition to be convenient for analysis of almost any size of possible observed pieces. The attributes of the polishes were assessed using 20x LMPLAN objective and 15x oculars. This magnification corresponds with the most appropriate magnification for general interpretation of polishes (Moss 1986; Gijn 1990) and provides the comparable visual phenomena (polish attributes description) with other analysts. The lower magnification (10x UMPLAN objective and 15x oculars) was used for scanning the piece for presence of polishes and examination of the wear location and its relation to the working edge. However, this magnification does not provide sufficient details to allow for interpreting of the polishes, except the extensive "sickle gloss" polishes.

Filters employed included a polarizing filter, blue and green filter and Nomarski DIC. All filters were tested for achieving the best results either for observation or microphotography. Although the blue and green filters were frequently used in previous studies to increase contrast, I did not find them as helpful as other analysts, probably also as the digital camera was employed instead of the classic photographic equipment. Also, Nomarski has not brought much additional value for observing flint/radiolarite/chert artefacts. However, it could be helpful for analyses of non flint materials. On the other hand, the polarizing filter was employed for almost all observations as it significantly decreases the negative effects of the white patina to surface observation. Although the microscope could switch to dark-field illumination, this option was not used for use-wear interpretation in this research.

The microphotographs were taken at first by an optical camera with an automatic light-exposure meter attached to microscope. However, this old system was very inefficient as the high number of photos of the analysed place must have been taken with a very unsure result. Unfortunately, the tool cannot be securely fixed under the objective so the micro-motions of the tool due to stone weight or other influences may occur during the exposure. As the exposure time is usually long the object often slowly moves out of focus. To minimize the exposure time it was necessary to use professional black-and-white films with a high sensitivity (e.g. Ilford Pan films, 200-400 ASA) and extremely fine grain and high resolution power. The films should have been developed in a special way and photos were, in an ideal case, processed by the analysts itself to receive the best results. The commercial photo development I found completely useless as the automatic photo development machines were not able to focus the relevant part of the photo. So, besides the problem with the focus during the microscopy, the photos were not sharp due to their incorrect development. This could be minimized by self development of photos but still the necessity to repeat photography of a desired place when any of the previously made snaps did not look proper was very frustrating and expensive. As the photo must have been made in a bulk to fill the film the repeating work after film development (after a necessary time delay) was time consuming.

Fortunately, during the research the technical development of digital cameras accelerated and this equipment started to be available for a reasonable price and also the chip resolution over 3 million of pixels is sufficient for the needs of this type of microphotography. The Olympus microscope allows direct attachment of the semi-professional Olympus digital cameras. Further, the external PixelView USB device + PlayTV USB Pro TV v1.18 software were used to transfer the image online to a computer display as there use to be a small difference in focus between standard oculars and the ocular for a camera. This device was not ideal due to a small resolution on PC display for focusing (320 x 240). Now, there are available much sophisticated solutions, for example Olympus QuickPHOTO MICRO 2.1. Unfortunately, the new photo equipment could have been used only at the very end of my work, for the Pavlov periphery analysis, so that the most of photographs in the previous researches are in a lower quality.

The microphotos were taken in a high quality JPEG format. Only a polarizing filter was used as any other filters significantly lowered the exposure time and removed some fine details, although they increased the contrast. However, this is not the highest priority for the digital photo anymore as contrast and other attributes can be adjusted immediately on the computer screen. Other advantage of digital photography is a possibility to magnify the analysed polish to the size which was not available with microscope oculars, i.e. obtain a higher magnification than 300x provided. I found it helpful for more detailed analysis of questionable cases of polish interpretation. However, this was possible only as additional information as the microphotos show only one horizontal plane and various topographical features of a polish spot may be out of focus. Therefore, it is still impossible to interpret use-wear traces solely on the basis of photographs, moreover, the distribution of the polish and its spatial relationship to the edges are transferable to the photograph only as a composition of several photos. There are now available software and devices capable of making a panoramic view of the large segment of analysed object or to make a "3D" picture by a composition of several following pictures with a different focus, but they are still too complicated and expensive for a widespread and routine practice of microwear analysis. But it is probable that the rapid technical development in these technologies will soon provide us with new possibilities regarding the microphotographs.

2.4 Data registration

The attributes of observed wear phenomena were registered in computer database system created in MS Access, inspired by the database systems used in other studies, mainly in Leiden laboratory. Van Gijn (1990) developed a complex system for registering data for a variety of assemblages, not only for those examined for the use-wear. The system I developed and used in this study did not require such complexity as it was used for the microwear analysis only. Therefore, the three-level hierarchical system (site-file, macro-file, micro-file; Gijn 1990) was modified to two-level system (artefact-data, micro-data).

The first level included variables concerning the entire artefact: artefact registration number, site, typology, morphology, raw material, grain size, fragment, artefact measurements, postdepositional modifications, cleaning procedures, photo registration, etc.

The second level included variables defined for all analysed areas of the artefact: location of observed phenomena, edge angle, LPA variables (edge removals (ER) attributes – ER location, ER distribution, ER termination, ER orientation, ER width, edge rounding), HPA variables (polish (PO) location, PO distribution, PO texture, PO brightness, PO topography, PO width, striation amount, PO/striations directionality) degree of wear, direction of motion, final interpretation separately for LPA (hardness category of contact material) and HPA (contact material). Every analysed artefact has at least one micro-data record, either the interpretation category "no traces" or the full description of the observed wear traces. The tool can have one or more used areas – the amount was not limited but it was rare to find more that two areas used for different activities. Such a result could appear due to three possible situations: the tool was hafted, tool was used more than once (either on the same or on different contact material, including retooling) or the various used areas could have been caused by one but complex activity/task. However, it is very problematic to differentiate between the last two categories. Unless the rich contextual archaeological data collection from the excavated site is available, it is impossible to link several used areas in a behaviourally meaningful way (cf. Gijn 1990).

For the description of the observed phenomena location, a coordinates system based on general tool shape was used. The artefact was oriented in dorsal position with the proximal end facing downwards. If the proximal-distal orientation could not be assessed, the orientation was based on a tool shape (longitudinal axis + the dominant "functional" end facing upwards. Every observed phenomenon was precisely registered to 1:1 tool picture. However, for the following computer comparison, the traces were located by either a single coordinate which was the closest to it or, if it extended to a wider space, by two marginal coordinates, for example the polish covering the whole left edge.

2.5 LPA

Low power approach (LPA) developed historically as a method dealing with the edge damages resulting from the use, especially with microscarring, using a low magnification. At this time the LPA method is usually involved as indivisible part of microwear analysis, providing extended information for HPA based interpretation. Although there are various problems which limit the interpretation of tool use solely on the basis of the edge damage, for example, the use retouch is difficult to distinguish from the intentional retouch or manufacturing, I was encouraged by Anne Louise van Gijn to make an independent record of the LPA attributes to evaluate the LPA possibility for the analysed Palaeolithic material. Therefore, the presence of edge removals (use retouch and edge rounding) was registered into database, including the detailed attributes of microscars: size, termination, location, direction.

The hardness of the worked materials was divided into three categories (cf. Odell and Odell-Vereecken 1980, see chapter 1.):

- hard materials (e.g. shells, bones, antlers, frozen materials, dry meat or dry hide)
- soft materials (e.g. soft vegetable material, fresh hide, fat and other soft animal tissues but clay for ceramic products could as well be involved)
- medium hard materials (e.g. wood, hard vegetable bulbs or roots, etc.)

However, the medium hard category is meant only as an auxiliary category and can be considered an intermediary stage between soft and hard materials, just for more exact classification.

Hide as a specific material can exist in all hardness categories, depending on the state of hide processing. The fresh hide represents a very soft but resilient material which during the following procedures of hide processing can change into a very hard and tough state (e.g. dry unprocessed hide). The other factor that may undoubtedly influence the hide hardness is the specie of the animal; understandably, different species have a different quality of hide (Anderson-Gefraud et al. 1987). Similar change of hardness of a worked material from hard to medium hard or even to soft can be achieved by soaking antler, bone and hard wood into water. In fact, these materials are almost un-manufacturable in a dry state.

The edge rounding, the other phenomenon observed using the LPA method and recorded to database, is mostly connected with hide-working (Gijn 1990) and can help to differentiate the contact material but the postdepositional modification must be considered.

The results of LPA were compared with the results received from the HPA method (see capture 7.8).

2.6 HPA

The used areas are usually located and preferably interpreted on the basis of a presence of the polish although the description of the use-polishes is the most intricate and subjective aspect of functional analysis, leaving aside the yet unfinished discussion about what constitutes the use-polish (see the chapter 1.). The methodology for recording HPA data of micropolishes was inspired by the one used in the Lithic Laboratory in Leiden. The data include various attributes such as brightness, distribution, texture and various topographical features (location, extent etc.) based on visual perception of polish topography – they have no bearings on the mechanics of the polish formation. Detailed descriptions of all attributes can be found in A.L. van Gijn's book (1990). However, I found the verbal descriptions used for the above mentioned attributes rather subjective and I suppose that for their "sharing" with other analysts it is necessary to consider the attributes personally, to be sure what the "real" meaning of the description is. Nevertheless, this does not reduce the possibility of the

polish interpretation; it is only more difficult to describe the polish "look" for the respective contact materials unlike the LPA where the description of observed attributes is much easier and more explicit.

The other phenomenon observed by HPA was striation. Striations are grooves and scratches of varying dimension. Some can be observed with a naked eye, while others are only visible at high magnifications in the optical microscope or in the SEM. Striations are thought to be caused by abrasive particles or grit and they can reflect a range of processes, including the natural phenomena (Juel Jensen 1988). Thus, while striations can be valuable indicators of use motion, they can be considered the result of intentional work only when accompanied by other wear traces (Keeley and Newcomer 1977). Although some analysts attempted to correlate morphological stria-types with worked materials (Semenov 1957; Mansur 1983; Mansur-Franchomme 1983) this research, as most of other studies (e.g.

Vaughan 1985a; Gijn 1990), used the appearance of striations, their orientation and their distribution on the tool surface, for the indication and interpretation of the working activity/motion only.

As I did not have the opportunity to use any instruments for a residues analysis, this category was not included into this research. Also, as most of the artefacts had been cleaned immediately after the excavation with the HCl to remove a coating of mineral deposits from loess sediments, the appearance and analysis of possible residues would be rather limited at any case because most of the residues disappear after immersion even in a light acidic solution (pH 5) (Gijn 1990).

2.7 Common variables

As mentioned above, the final interpretation was made separately for the LPA and HPA method. But this does not necessarily mean that they were in contradiction. If both types of traces are present, both interpretations can be made, the HPA interpretation represents the type of worked material while LPA interpretation indicates its state at the time it was worked.

The development of use-wear traces is influenced by several factors (see chapters 1.2 and 2.9): the raw material, contact material, motion, duration of work, exerted pressure, intensity of work, worker's experience, etc. Therefore, all these variables cannot be interpreted as duration of work but rather as the degree of wear. This value includes also the factor of postdepositional surface modification which further influences the preservation of the use-wear traces, i.e. the analyst's certainty of the use-wear traces interpretation.

The categories used for description of the degree of wear and the certainty degrees were set as follows:

- no traces
- not interpretable
- unsure (50% certainty that the traces are from the use)
- probably used (75% certainty that the traces are from the use)

- lightly worn (99% certainty that the traces are from the use)
- lightly + possibly resharpened (99% certainty that the traces are from the use)
- medium worn (99% certainty that the traces are from the use)
- heavily worn (99% certainty that the traces are from the use)

The motion of the tool during the work was interpreted and concluded for both methods, LPA and HPA, if the directionality attributes were available (orientation of scars, PO/striations direction). The description of a direction of the motion is related to the used edge. Due to the lack of contextual information about the excavated sites and the working activities carried out in Palaeolithic in general, the motions were strictly divided into basic geometrical directions (longitudinal, transversal, diagonal), although they could be associated with a specific working activity. Together with the contact material interpretation, the personal judgment on activity could be made but I felt the implicit name should not be included in the concluding interpretation as, mainly due to the character of a wear preservation, this cannot be taken for granted.

2.8 Cleaning

The examined tools had to be cleaned before the microscopic analysis to remove superficial impurities that may cover the use-wear traces during the observation. The cleaning of implements prior examination constitutes an essential, but much debated, part of the microwear research. There are several approaches to cleaning methods of the prehistoric tools.

Some analysts have the opinion that it is necessary to clean the analysed tool very carefully, using alcohol, warm detergent solution, chemicals (10% HCl to remove minerals deposits/carbonate encrustation and 20-30% KOH to remove organic residues) and ultrasonic bath (Keeley 1980). The series of all steps is extremely time consuming and therefore the procedure is often simplified, for instance by using only HCl. Also, the 5%-35% solution of H_2O_2 can be used to simulate the effects of diagenesis or burial (Anderson 1980; Jahren et al 1997; Derndarsky and Ocklind 2001) or 5% NH_4OH (Evans and Donahue 2005).

On the other side, some scientists suppose that Palaeolithic and Mesolithic industry should not be cleaned with chemicals at all (unless they are covered with a coating of mineral deposits) as some results have indicated the vulnerability of polishes to a chemical attack (e.g. Plisson 1986; Plisson and Mauger 1988). The scientists stress that the ancient artefacts were deposited for a long time in soil matrix, where they were exposed to natural chemical solutions, so a minimum of the original organic remains could be preserved or fixed on the tool surface. Therefore, further use of chemicals would be redundant or even more harmful (Gijn 1990; Juel Jensen 1994; Levi-Sala 1996).

The cleaning is also necessary from the point of a definition what constitutes a "polish". The most satisfactory seems to be modified Vaughan's definition of micro-polish as "an altered flint surface which reflects light and which cannot be removed with weak acids, bases and solvents" (Gijn 1990; Moss 1986). This indicates that in some cases the cleaning is necessary, otherwise not polish but residues would be observed and the interpretation could be misleading (e.g. Bettison 1985). However, there is not enough knowledge about the polish structure and about their long-term reaction to chemical solution. Although, the polishes appear not to change in the optical microscope, the effect of chemical cleaning can prevent future application of more powerful and precise measuring techniques than the optical ones (Andersen and Whitlow 1983).

Considering all the above opinions and experiments, I decided that a detergent solution, alcohol and low concentration of HCl solution (if necessary) should be sufficient for the microwear analysis of prehistoric tools. I rejected the usage of hydroxides due to their ability to etch/dissolve silica and their contribution to white patina formation, although some researchers use them for removing the residues. However, every time the raw material and artefacts condition must be considered independently to avoid a possible damage of the surface. Especially Palaeolithic tools should be cleaned without

using a high concentration of chemicals as they can remove lightly developed polishes preserved on the surface or accelerate the development of postdepositional modifications such as patina which in the end also disables the polish observation. Acids could have a negative influence on use-wear traces observation as low pH can cause a postdepositional sheen (Rottländer 1975a, 1975b).

All analysed tools were cleaned before the analysis by using a weak cleaning solution (lukewarm soap/detergent water) and consecutively saturated by immersing in water for 15 minutes. Saturation was done because most artefacts had a secondary coating of mineral deposits and therefore cleaning by a weak solution (less than 5 %) of HCl was necessary (for 2-5 min). Water saturation should lower or inhibit the penetration of HCl into a stone surface and prevent the delayed development of sheen. It was ascertained that chemicals will continue to work on the structure if penetrate into a stone surface (Gijn 1990; Juel Jensen 1994). After the use of HCl the tools were rinsed under water current and once more immersed into detergent water to neutralize possible remains of acid. Used weak chemical solutions should have not caused any removal or alteration of micro-polishes. Higher concentrations or other solutions were not used. Before and during the microscopic analysis the tools were cleaned by 80% ethanol and cotton wool tampons to remove fingerprints. Acetone was used only to remove lacquer which covered the evidence number.

On the other side, the fresh experimental tool should be cleaned in chemical solution(s) to remove the residues and juices of worked materials that are strongly bound to a tool surface. If they are not completely removed they can falsify the observed appearance of use-wear polishes. Further, the usage of chemical solutions to some extend simulates the conditions of a tool that would have been deposited in soil matrix and similarly affects the developed experimental traces accordingly to the processes the ancient tools were exposed to.

2.9 Postdepositional modification

All irreversible surface modifications/damages which are not connected to the tool manufacture or usage are considered to be the postdepositional modifications. Most of them start to affect the surface after the tool functional life, but exceptions can occur. The main "natural" causes are compaction of the soil, trampling, soil creep, water transport, matrix chemistry etc. Therefore, some analysts require the analysed assemblage to be derived from primary context only (i.e. not superficial excavations) (cf.

Keeley 1980; Gijn 1990). However, this demand does not exclude the presence of postdepositional modifications although it lowers the probability of their appearance.

The presence of postdepositional modifications usually cannot be judged with the naked eye only. Except the white patina, heavy burning or extreme abrasion, the modifications change the microstructure of the surface which manifests as a different light reflection in microscope. So, the natural abrasion or sheen can occur even on assemblages which seemed to be of a fresh condition when examined with the naked eye (e.g. Mansur-Franchomme 1983; Moss 1983a). Therefore, it is necessary to get accustomed to the postdepositional alternation unique for each site while examining the first approximately 50 pieces, for which the interpretation must be later reconsidered (cf. Moss 1983a).

Logically, as due to the assemblage age, the surface of all Palaeolithic tools, depending on the assemblage age, was always more or less affected by postdepositional modification which can differ not just among the excavated sites but also within the artefacts from the same excavation. However, there is not a clear linear dependency between the artefact age and the degree of postdepositional modification. In some cases of very ancient tools, which could be supposed unsuitable for use-wear analysis, their surface can be in a better condition than those from much younger periods. On the contrary, the processes of a tool deposition in a specific matrix seem to play the main role together with the local chemical and climatic effects that may affect relatively small region. The degree of postdepositional modification can also differ not only among the artefacts from one excavated site but also within one artefact itself. For example, one side of an artefact was affected with a heavy patina but the surface on the opposite side looked almost fresh. Or, some edges were rounded by abrasion and the others were sharp. Such a phenomenon was described on different excavated Palaeolithic sites of a different age and probably is connected with the speed by which the artefacts were covered with sediments (e.g. Gijn 1990; Roebroeks et al. 1997; Šajnerová 2003b).

All artefacts, in here presented researches, derived from primary contexts, but a different time has elapsed since they were excavated, so the post-excavation alteration must have been tested. The most common observed postdepositional modifications were light abrasion, white patina, sheen and bright spots. The assemblages varied in age but all were embedded in alkaline matrixes – the loess-derived sediments or karts sediments so the chemical alteration should be of a similar type. That explains the presence of a high degree of white patina on most analysed flint/chert tools.

White patina is a chemical alteration of the stone surface which manifests as a thin layer of whitish colouration covering (part of) a tool. The surface of white patinated flint/chert appears as porous and reflects light to all directions. Most authors agree that alkaline environments induce the white patina; its formation can be reproduced experimentally in various alkaline solutions with pH of 10 or higher (Schmalz 1960; Rottländer 1975a, 1975b; Plisson 1986). The process of patination is connected with a slight weight loss, which is partly caused by dehydration of the chemical microstructure of a raw material (Schmalz 1960; Andersen and Whitlow 1983; Gijn 1990). Sometimes the formation of white patina is initiated also by the exposure to light, provided that the previous conditions were present but the patina has not appeared yet, for example during the excavation (Rottländer 1975b; Gijn 1990). Other conditions playing role in white patina formation, not connected to the matrix chemical nature, seem to be desiccation and exposure to a combined effect of sun, dew and temperature differences typical for hot climates which eventually lead to the total disintegration of the smaller artefacts (Texier 1981; Gijn 1990). However, dissolution of silica can be caused just by leaching the artefacts by a flow of pure water (pH 7) or degraded by a silicophage bacteria whose role in desilicification of flints is probably underestimated (Plisson and Mauger 1988).

Unlike the flint/chert, the radiolarite artefacts were not affected by white patina, probably due to their different material microstructure. But their surface was modified with soil sheen, which origin has not been well understood yet (Rottländer 1975a, 1975b; Stapert 1976; Gijn 1990). I suppose that the sheen could be present also on the white patinated flint tools but its effect was conjoined in white patina optical interference.

Beside patina, the appearance and variability of so-called bright spots on analysed assemblages could be very interesting. The origin of "bright spots" or a "friction gloss" is not clear at present. They are supposed to develop by a contact with other silicates or minerals (e.g. Shepherd 1972), or they can be in some cases an indication of hafting traces (Stapert 1976; Moss 1987b; Gijn 1990) although of the same origin, i.e. crushed stone particles in a haft binder or interspace. Bright spots were quite common on the analysed chipped industry and they were characterised by a high brightness, smooth polish texture and flat topography. But despite their size and extension, those spots were in fact isolated and located at position which did not correspond with the anticipated location of the use-wear traces on the working edges. Moreover, the polish intensity was too high considering the age of artefacts. Other diagnostic feature which usually distinguishes bright spots from the regular use-wear polishes is missing directionality, i.e. the polish does not have any significant features which would refer to movement of the tool along the worked material. But this is not a dogma as extensive (use-like) bright spots with a clear directionality were observed on the analysed Lower Palaeolithic assemblage from Stránská skála (Šajnerová 2003b, Valoch and Šajnerová 2005).

The mechanical alternations of artefacts, light abrasion and postdepositional edge scarring, used to be a result of compaction of the soil, trampling, soil creep or the excavation and post-excavation activities. As the nature of the soil matrix, except the Karst assemblage, was more or less the same for the analysed artefacts, I could compare the influence of post-excavation damage of the Pavlov artefacts excavated in 1954-71 and Dolní Věstonice assemblage excavated in 1999. I have not observed any significant difference either in degree of patination, edge-scarring or abrasion between assemblages from those two sites or among the individual excavations in Pavlov site (i.e. 1954, 1957, 1970 and 1971).

Fortunately, the Research Center for Paleolithic and Paleoethnology in Dolní Věstonice (Institute of Archaeology ASCR Brno) treats their recent excavations with the respect that the artefacts could be analysed for use-wear traces and neither of the previously excavated assemblages were critically damaged by the post-excavation activities, but I would still like to recapitulate several recommendations (based both on other analysts' advices and my own experience) regarding the artefact handling to be suitable for use-wear analysis:

1. Avoid using the metal screen for sieving as it produces irremovable metal polish.
2. Avoid an intensive rubbing off the adhering sediments as this can produce abrasion of the artefacts surface and the use-polishes can be removed. If possible, the cleaning should be done under a water current with as little rubbing as possible.
3. Avoid using pencil on artefact surface. The graphite makes a hardly removable layer on the most important parts of edges which hides any possible polish located there (Fig. 6-2).

4. Place the evidence numbers outside the possible used areas, far away from the edges. The numbering with the ink and nail-polish does not cause any lasting damage but it takes a lot of extra time when it has to be removed from the analysed area and replaced to another, more suitable area.
5. Avoid using NaOH for cleaning artefacts as it causes an intensive desiccation of the silicate structure. If necessary to use HCl, soak the implements in water prior the acid application and then follow by rinsing with tap water and neutralize the remains with a weak base (detergent water). The acids can cause a bluish sheen or yellow colouration of the surface.
6. Avoid contact among artefacts (storing in large bags) as it causes extensive edge damages (which can remove the existing polish), friction gloss, linear streaks of polish, slight rounding of edges and ridges. If possible, put the retouched pieces in own bags. If refitting is concerned, it is better to leave it until wear trace analysis has been performed.
7. Avoid scattering of large bags of flints onto table as it could cause extensive edge damages or artefacts fracture. Avoid repeated handling of implements in hands as it produces a meat-like polish. Therefore, the assemblage should not be used as "study-collection" prior the wear trace analysis was performed.

I am aware that it is not always possible to follow all the above mentioned recommendations but if it is done, there is much higher possibility of preserving the use-wear traces for further observations.

3. Pavlov I (excavation 1954, 1957, 1970-71)

Pavlov I represents a typical settlement in the Moravian Gravettian landscape as defined by J. Svoboda (2005), which differs from the Aurignacian or Magdalenian landscapes. Gravettian sites in Moravia were related to the riverine networks and localized on the valley slopes and elevations in relatively low altitudes 200-300 m a.s.l. In the area, the sites were distributed in almost regular distances (Svoboda 1999, 2005). Formation of the large hunter's settlements is a characteristic phenomenon of the Gravettian in Moravia (e.g. Předmostí I, Dolní Věstonice I, Pavlov I). These mega-sites are characteristic with their size (min. diameter of 100 m), the density of artefacts, thickness of cultural layers and charcoal deposits and complexity of activities. According to faunal analysis (Musil 2005) and the lithic industry (Verpoorte 2005) it seems the occupation of this site was of a permanent or semi-permanent character, with emphasis on the winter season.

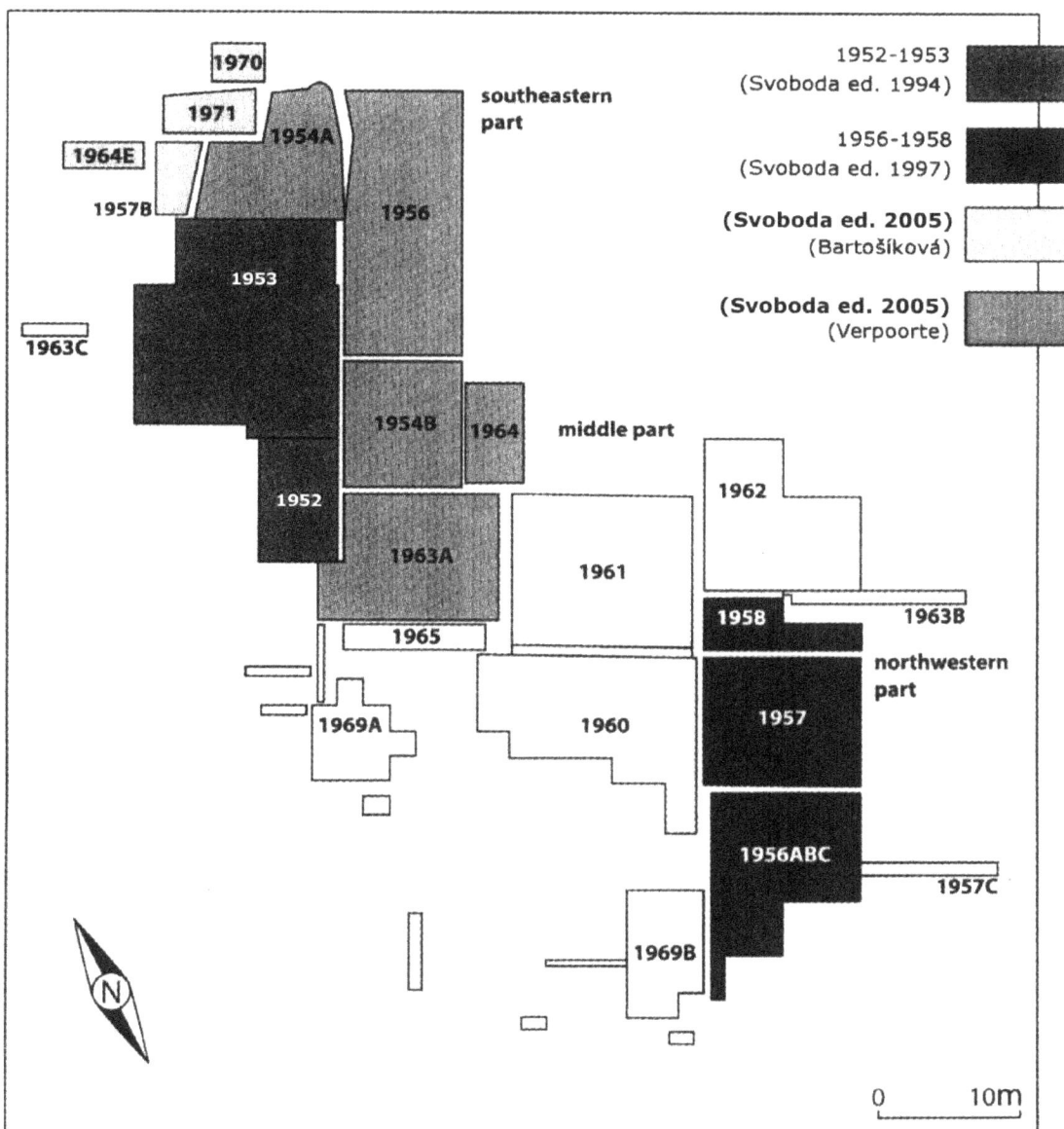

Fig. 3-1 General plan of the Pavlov I excavations, by Klíma and Verpoorte (2005).

Bohuslav Klíma opened excavation in Pavlov during the 1950s and the research continued until 2004, when the international team of researchers completed a long-term multidisciplinary process of description and evaluation of the site and its inventories (Svoboda, ed. 1994 - Pavlov I: excavation 1952-53; Svoboda, ed. 1997 - Pavlov I – Northwest: excavation 1957-58; Svoboda, ed. 2005 - Pavlov I – Southeast: excavations 1954, 1956-7, 1963-4, 1970-1). Comparable to other excavations made in those times, the data set was based on a 1 m square grid recording system so the data for more detailed microstratigraphy (individual, three-dimensional artefact records) are not available.

The findings of human burials, carvings in ivory, the ceramic production, traces of colorants suggest that Pavlov and the near site Dolní Věstonice were the centres for activities related to rituals, information storage and transmission by the means of symbols, decoration of bodies and their ritual deposition in graves. Those traces of symbolism place Pavlov together with Dolní Věstonice on the top of the site-hierarchy not only quantitatively but also qualitatively as the places for special activities (Svoboda 2005).

The decision to make a comparative approach of the older excavations of the densely settled area (excavation 1954-6) and the peripheral areas (excavation 1957, 1970 and 1971) provided a great opportunity to apply a set of new and modern methods to this exceptional settlement not only in Europe but worldwide. It was decided to select from the incredible amount of found implements only sample groups for use-wear analysis. The aim of the analysis was to prove the best approach in applying use-wear analysis on this material and to evaluate the adequacy of using both methods - the High Power Approach (HPA) and the Low Power Approach (LPA). The second task was to decide whether there had been any differences between using tools made from two major raw materials (radiolarite, flint). The results were compared with the results from other sites with the focus on the interpreted use-wear traces and the length of settlement. Finally, the intention was to check whether one of those raw materials would be more suitable for the analysis, considering the high patination of flints.

The final monograph "Pavlov I Southeast: A window into the Gravettian lifestyles" (Svoboda, ed.) including the microwear analysis results was published in Dolní Věstonice Series 14 (Šajnerová 2005).

3.1 Material and sampling

All provided assemblages are property of the Research Center for Paleolithic and Paleoethnology in Dolní Věstonice, the Institute of Archaeology ASCR in Brno. The analysed tools consisted of four sample groups according to the excavations: excavation in 1954A – 161 pieces, excavation in 1957 – 112 pieces, excavation in 1970 – 63 pieces, excavation in 1971 – 108 pieces. Considering the raw materials, the samples consisted of 79% (352 pieces) of flint and 21% (92 pieces) of radiolarite. The distribution of the raw materials in each sample is presented in Tab. 3-1.

Tab. 3-1 Composition of the raw materials in the analysed samples.

Raw material	1954A	1957	1970	1971	Total
Flint	93	104	61	94	352
Radiolarite	68	8	2	14	92
Total	161	112	63	108	444

Detailed typology of the analysed implements was done by A. Verpoorte (2005) and Z. Bartošíková (2005). However, for further analysis the tools were divided into more general typological groups (Tab. 3-2).

Tab. 3-2 Composition of the typological groups in the analysed samples.

Typology group	1954A	1957	1970	1971	Total
Blades	33%	60%	49%	44%	45%
Burins	12%	13%	16%	19%	15%
Combi	2%	3%	2%	5%	3%
Flakes	12%	4%	6%	2%	7%
Chisels	3%	0%	0%	2%	2%
Microliths	20%	4%	6%	7%	11%
Points	3%	0%	0%	1%	1%
Scrapers	11%	15%	17%	13%	13%
Others	4%	3%	3%	6%	4%

The sample of the excavation from 1954A represents the central settled area. On the contrary, the samples of the excavations in 1957, 1970 and 1971 seemed to lie on the settlement periphery. Considering the archaeological context during the excavations (bones, fire places, living objects etc.), all the peripheries looked very similar. Neither did the typological group compositions of the analysed industry show any major differences. There was only a significantly higher amount of flakes and microliths in the sample from the central area (Pavlov 1954A) than at the peripheries.

The analysed samples did not display any obvious differences in the typological structure between flints and radiolarites, only the microliths were more often made from flint. However, this difference could only be a result of the selection of flint artefacts as explained below.

The selection of the analysed sample groups was of two types: the complete selection of all inventoried chipped pieces from a selected area (central settlement area, excavation 1954A) and the selection carried out under more restrictive criteria (settlement periphery areas, excavation 1957, 1970 and 1971). It is important to bear in mind that all chipped pieces were already pre-selected by excavators during the respective excavations and only the bigger or retouched pieces/tools were selected for inventorying. The vast majority of the stone artefacts, consisting primarily of small debitage, were stored collectively according to the excavation year. The sample pieces were selected only from the inventoried collection, the bulk material was not analysed. According to A. Verpoorte (2005) the inventoried pieces from the excavation in 1954 comprised about 5% of all the excavated pieces! Therefore, the percentage data of the analysed samples must be considered only as illustrative.

During the excavations the found objects were documented by squares. Due to the enormous number of the excavated industry found in the central area of the settlement during the excavation in 1954, it was decided to make a complete sample of all chipped industry inventoried in pre-selected squares. The cultural layer reached 40 cm in some of the squares and it is supposed

that it originated from several subsequent settlements. Therefore, from the central settlement area (excavation 1954A) the squares 7/I and 7/II were chosen for use-wear analysis as they displayed a relatively thin layer of settlement, where all implements could be from the same settlement period. The assumption was also made that those squares did not represent exclusive working areas as the incidence of tool types corresponded with the tool type percentage in the whole collection. The second sample from the central settlement was created as a complete selection of all radiolarite implements inventoried during the excavation in 1954A.

The samples from the periphery sites (excavations from 1957, 1970 and 1971) were pre-selected by specific restrictive criteria: all retouched pieces or those pieces with a straight edge over 1 cm in length were selected for microanalysis. The primary collections of the inventoried pieces before the selection were: excavation from 1957 - 520 pieces, excavation from 1970 - 261 pieces and excavation from 1971 - 923 pieces. This indicates that the pre-selected pieces (considered as probably used) in total amount of 283 pieces made up about 12-24% of all the chipped industry found at the peripheries. Moreover, according to Z. Bartošíková (2005) the inventoried pieces from the excavation in 1957 comprised about 25% of all the excavated pieces and 30% from the excavations in 1970 and 1971. This must be taken into account during the interpretation (see chapter 7.7)

3.2 Results and discussion

Since the very beginning the results have been divided according to the expected settlement location - central area versus the periphery. In the central area samples, 51 pieces from 161 analysed implements showed no use-wear traces, which made up about 32%; from the material point of view 44% of the flint and 14% of the radiolarite artefacts had no interpretable traces. The apparently higher percentage of unused flint implements was caused by a higher amount of microliths in comparison to the radiolarite artefacts (28 flint and 6 radiolarite microliths). It seems that the microliths make up a specific group in the microanalysis (to be discussed later). Unfortunately, the entire material was highly affected by postdepositional modifications, mainly white patina, which contributed to the lower interpretability of the analysis. Due to this fact, 10 pieces (6%) had traces of possible use but neither the contact material nor the motion could be interpreted by using the LPA or HPA methods. Interpretable signs of use-wear were traced on 100 pieces (62%).

Similarly, a total of 163 pieces from the 283 analysed implements of the periphery samples showed no use-wear traces, which is about 58%; 23 pieces (8%) had uninterpretable traces by both the LPA and HPA methods and 97 pieces (34%) showed interpretable signs of use-wear at least by one method. However, it is necessary to recalculate the results with regards to the primary samples from which the analysed pieces were pre-selected. Then, the real percentage of used pieces would be on average only about 7% of all the inventoried pieces (compared to 61% from the central area). Further, there seem to be some differences in the peripheral researches. The detailed comparison of the results of each peripheral excavation sample revealed that the excavated area in 1971 differed from those in 1957 and 1970. Firstly, the number of retouched pieces was lower than in the two other peripheries (only about 8%) and secondly, only 3% of the inventoried pieces showed clear traces of use (Tab. 3-3). It is also noticeable that there were significant differences in the percentage of the used retouched pieces among the peripheral samples.

23

Tab. 3-3 Degree of the interpreted use-wear traces plus a composition of the retouched pieces in the analysed samples.

Excavation	Central	Periphery		
	1954	1957	1970	1971
Retouched pieces	47%	66% (14%)	52% (13%)	69% (8%)
% of used retouched pieces	70%	59%	85%	38%
Use-wear traces				
Not interpretable	6%	9% (2%)	14% (3%)	4% (1%)
Interpretable traces	62%	37% (8%)	45% (11%)	25% (3%)
No traces	32%	54% (90%)	41% (86%)	71% (96%)

Notes:
x% - values of analysed samples
(x%) - recalculated values for the primary samples of the pre-selected peripheral excavations, the 1954A sample was analysed as a whole

In comparison, Silvia Tomášková (1994) conducted use-wear analysis of the chipped industry from the excavation in 1952-3 using only the LPA method. She interpreted 42% of the implements as having been used. This excavation is supposed to be located in the central area of the settled area. We can also compare the results with another excavated Gravettian site, the Dolní Věstonice excavation in 1999, where only 12% of the found implements were interpreted as having been used (see following chapter, Tab.4-2). The Dolní Věstonice 1999 excavation was considered a short term settlement and the low percentage of used tools corresponded with that. Although, the results of the short term settlement may resemble the Pavlov periphery sample results, the typological structure was different (for example there were no scrapers excavated in Dolní Věstonice in 1999) and probably the reason for the low percentage of used tools would be different too. This is also indicated by the explicit result of the degree of development of the found use-wear traces (Tab. 3-4, cf. Tab. 4-3).

Both the central and the peripheral areas had a very similar composition of the degree of development of the traces interpreted on the used pieces, except the slight difference in the 1971 excavation - probably caused by the very small amount of used pieces altogether. On the

contrary, in the Dolní Věstonice 1999 excavation no extensively used tools were found (Tab. 4-3).

Tab. 3-4 Degree of development of the interpreted use-wear traces.

Degree of traces	Central	Periphery		
	1954	1957	1970	1971
Unsure/ Possible use	60%	36%	41%	29%
Light use	14%	32%	22%	32%
Medium use	19%	26%	31%	29%
Extensive use	7%	6%	6%	11%

Some of the examined artefacts could have had more than one used area or could have been retooled – the rest of the originally used areas could still be visible. In 17 instances two actually used areas (AUAs) and in 3 instances even three AUAs were interpreted from the 100 used pieces; in most cases either blades (with both edges used) or burins. Supernumerary AUAs were found more often on radiolarite than flint implements and they were usually of an unsure degree. The periphery samples had supernumerary AUAs interpreted less frequently; only 12 instances (from 97 used pieces) had two AUAs.

Tab. 3-5 Distribution of the tool fragments and the location of the use-wear traces.

Fragment	Central		Periphery	
	% of analysed sample	% of used fragments	% of analysed sample	% of used fragments
Complete	35%	61%	43%	47%
Distal	32%	83%	22%	62%
Medial	7%	71%	10%	37%
Proximal	20%	82%	21%	31%
Unsure	5%	60%	4%	33%

Tab. 3-6 Interpretation of the use-wear traces using a binocular microscope (LPA) in the central area.

Central 1954A						
Typology group	Hard material	Medium material	Soft material	Unsure	Total AUAs	No traces (pieces)
Blades	7	14	13	24	58	10
Burins	8	3	1	7	19	7
Combi	1		2	1	4	
Flakes	1	2	6	4	13	7
Chisels	3	1			4	1
Microliths			1	4	5	29
Others			2	2	4	3
Points	1			1	2	5
Scrapers	1	1	9	5	16	2
Total count	22	21	34	48	125	64
% of total AUAs	18%	17%	27%	38%		
Total % of analysed pieces	14%	13%	21%	30%		40%

Tab. 3-7 Interpretation of the use-wear traces using a binocular microscope (LPA) in the peripheral areas.

Periphery (1957, 1970, 1971)						
Typology group	Hard material	Medium material	Soft material	Unsure	Total AUAs	No traces (pieces)
Blades		17	28	13	58	95
Burins		3	4	5	12	34
Combi		2	7	1	10	1
Flakes			1		1	9
Chisels					0	2
Microliths				4	4	14
Others				2	2	10
Points					0	1
Scrapers		2	36	2	40	4
Total count	0	24	76	27	127	170
% of total AUAs	0%	19%	60%	21%		
Total % of analysed pieces	0%	8%	27%	10%		60%

The distribution of the tool fragments in the analysed samples was almost equal in the central area, i.e. the complete, distal and proximal fragments made about one third each. However, the traces were observed more often on the distal and proximal fragments than on the complete tools. This could be influenced by the fact that microliths with mostly no traces found made up a significant part of the complete tools. A slightly different situation was found in the periphery samples where complete tools made up over 40% and the traces were mostly located on the distal fragments (Tab.3-5).

The overview of the interpreted traces categorized by the hardness of the worked material (LPA) is presented in Tab. 3-6 and Tab. 3-7 and the overview of the traces interpreted by the incident light microscope (HPA) is presented in Tab. 3-8 and Tab. 3-9. In the central area sample, both materials (flint and radiolarite) had very similar distribution in the hardness of the worked materials (LPA). The small differences between flints and radiolarites found in the worked materials (HPA) could have probably been more influenced by the different surface alteration than by real differences or by the selective use of tools made from one material for a specific activity. The prevalent worked material for both radiolarite and flint was hide (Fig. 3-4 till Fig. 3-8). It accounted for about 51% of all traces interpreted by the HPA method. Traces on two of the radiolarite blades were interpreted as "polish 10" (Gijn 1997, Fig. 3-3) or "hide-like polish" (Juel Jensen 1994), which used to be described as a well developed rough matt bright polish with a lot of deep striations resembling either to hide or plant polish and has not been reproduced experimentally yet.

If we compare the central and the periphery samples, obviously, in the central area the industry displayed a higher percentage of used tools than in the peripheries (Tab. 3-3). However, the most apparent difference was in the presence of the hard material use-wear traces, which were quite rare in the periphery samples (Fig. 3-2 and 3-9). This could be explained in two ways: hard materials were for some reason worked more often in the central

area of the settlement; and/or the development of the hard material traces takes longer to be visible on the tool surface. As to the degree of trace developed on tools from the periphery, the samples displayed more of the lightly developed traces (Tab. 3-4). This indicates that the majority of the tools were used only for a short period and therefore the hard material traces could not have been developed enough to be observed. We should consider a combination of both reasons as the most probable explanation.

Tab. 3-8 Interpretation of the worked materials using an incident light microscope (HPA) in the central area.

Typology group	Antler/ ivory bone/ wood	Soft animal material	Hide	Polish 10	Minerals	Unsure	Total AUAs	No traces (pieces)
Blades	2	4	26	2		17	51	17
Burins	5		4			10	19	7
Combi			3			1	4	
Flakes	1		5			6	12	8
Chisels						2	2	3
Microliths		1	4		1	2	8	26
Others			2			1	3	4
Points			2			1	3	4
Scrapers	2		15			1	18	
Total count	10	5	61	2	1	41	120	69
% of total AUAs	8%	4%	51%	2%	1%	34%		
Total % of analysed pieces	6%	3%	38%	1%	1%	25%		43%

Although Tomášková (2000) reported a significant portion of the plan working traces (30% of the interpreted traces on the Pavlov 1952-53 assemblage and about 20% of the working traces on the assemblage from the Willendorf II/layer 8), no such traces were observed on the analysed tools from these samples.

The direction of the tool motion during use was interpreted according to the direction of microscars and/or polish+striations. The description of the direction is related to the used edge (Tab. 3-10 and Tab. 3-11). The most frequent direction of the working motion in all samples partly corresponds with the typological groups. In the central area sample, the most frequent direction was the longitudinal motion (43% of the interpreted traces; 37% of the analysed tools); this is probably due to the predominance of blades in the analysed sample (33% of the analysed tools, Tab. 3-2). The second most

frequent motion was transversal, mostly scraping (26% of the interpreted traces; 22% of the analysed tools). Both motions were closely related to the process of hide-working.

Similarly, the Dolní Věstonice 1999 excavation had the longitudinal motion (about 37% of the interpreted traces) as the most frequent one, but contrary to the Pavlov I excavation, other motions (transversal, diagonal, hafting and boring) had almost equal but low frequency (Šajnerová 2001). This fact may indicate the correlation between specific activities and the duration of the settlement.

The peripheral samples indicated a slight predominance of the transversal motion (43% of the interpreted traces; 20% of the analysed tools) over the longitudinal motion (37% of the interpreted traces; 18% of the analysed tools), but this was probably caused by a higher percentage of scrapers in the peripheral samples than in the central area sample. Almost identical results reported Tomášková (2000) for her analysis of Pavlov assemblage from the excavation 1952-1953. Generally, the appearance of use-wear traces on the scrapers was more significant than on the blades, even though there were over 3x more blades than scrapers.

The comparison of the results of the different raw materials did not reveal any special preference in the selection of flint and radiolarite tools for different purposes or activities. Another interesting outcome of the study was that the typology of the tools highly correlated with an anticipated function/motion (Tab. 3-10 and Tab. 3-11).

Tab. 3-9 Interpretation of the worked materials using an incident light microscope (HPA) in the peripheral areas.

Typology group	Periphery (1957, 1970, 1971)						
	Unspecified hard material/ wood	Soft animal material	Hide	Minerals	Unsure	Total AUAs	No traces (pieces)
Blades	2	3	19	2	26	52	101
Burins		1	4		7	12	34
Combi			8		2	10	1
Flakes	1		1			2	8
Chisels						0	2
Microliths						0	18
Others					3	3	9
Points						0	1
Scrapers	2		31		8	41	3
Total count	5	4	63	2	46	120	177
% of total AUAs	4%	3%	53%	2%	38%		
Total % of analysed pieces	2%	1%	22%	1%	16%		63%

Tab. 3-10 Interpretation of the working motions in the central area.

Typology group	1954A	Direction of working material							
	Boring/ piercing	Diagonal	Dynamic activities	Longitudinal	Transverse.	Hafting	Unsure	Total AUAs	No traces (pieces)
Blades		1		42	4	6	8	61	7
Burins	1	7		5	2	2	4	21	5
Combi				1	1		2	4	
Flakes				4	6		3	13	7
Chisels					4			4	1
Microliths	1			5	1		2	9	25
Others				1	2	1		4	3
Points			1	2			1	4	3
Scrapers					16	1	1	18	
Total count	2	8	1	60	36	10	21	138	51
% of total AUAs	1%	6%	1%	43%	26%	7%	15%		
Total % of analysed pieces	1%	5%	1%	37%	22%	6%	13%		32%

Tab. 3-11 Interpretation of the working motion in the periphery samples.

Peripheries	Direction of working material							
Typology group	Boring/ piercing	Diagonal	Longitudinal	Transverse.	Hafting	Unsure	Total AUAs	No traces (pieces)
Blades	2	1	42	6	5	6	62	91
Burins			6	3		3	12	34
Combi			1	8		1	10	1
Flakes				1		1	2	8
Chisels							0	2
Microliths						4	4	14
Others			1			2	3	9
Points							0	1
Scrapers				40	1		41	3
Total count	2	1	50	58	6	17	134	163
% of total AUAs	1%	1%	37%	43%	4%	13%		
Total % of analysed pieces	1%	0%	18%	20%	2%	6%		58%

Parallel with use-wear analysis, the angle of the used edge was measured. The typological groups seemed to have a specific range of angles of the used edge, which were probably the most effective for the respective activity (Tab. 3-12).

Tab. 3-12 Angle of the used edges (all samples).

Typology group (flint/radiolarite)	0 - 30°	31° - 60°	61° - 90°	> 90°
Blades	16/6	54/35	1/2	1/-
Burins	2/-	5/7	7/6	1/-
Chisels		2/-	6/-	
Combi	1/-	2/1	2/3	1/-
Flakes	3/1	4/3	2/1	-/1
Microliths	-/2	4/1	3/2	
Other	1/-	2/-	2/1	
Points	-/1	-/2		
Scrapers		13/2	30/11	1/-
Total count	23/10	86/51	54/26	4/1

The average angle of the flint blades was 39° and was similar to the radiolarite blades (40°). Noticeably, the radiolarite blades appeared to have a more uniform angle (StDev 10,6) than the flint blades (StDev 13,8). Likewise the blades, the flint and radiolarite scrapers displayed a high similarity in angles. The radiolarite scrapers had on average almost identical angles as the flint scrapers (average 68°). However, the angles of the scrapers were again much more uniform for radiolarites (StDev 5,4) than for flints (StDev 12,4).

All flint artefacts showed a high to medium degree of white patina that lowered the possibility of interpretation using the incident light microscope (as already mentioned above). As most of the flint implements were heavily modified by the presence of white patina, there was a notion to continue only with use-wear analysis on radiolarites, which are rarely patinated. Unfortunately, the radiolarite implements were also influenced by a postdepositional modification of the surface (gloss patina), which together with the natural appearance of crystals in the radiolarite structure made the HPA method even more difficult.

The other frequent postdepositional modifications common to both flints and radiolarites were bright spots (aka friction gloss) and (similarly to Dolní Věstonice) black residual spots of an unknown origin. The comparison of postdepositional modifications found on the stored material from Pavlov I excavated from 50s to 70s and the newly excavated Gravettian site – Dolní Věstonice II (excavation in 1999) did not show any significant differences, which means that the postdepositional modifications were not caused by the long storage of the material (Šajnerová 2001).

3.3 Conclusion

The Gravettian settlement in Pavlov represented a great opportunity to apply microwear analysis on the chipped industry and reveal the real activities conducted at the site. The exclusiveness of the found artefacts led some archaeologists to use Pavlovian as an independent name for this regional archaeological culture. Thus, microwear analysis could extend our knowledge not only about this important site but also the Gravettian culture in general.

Considering the possible interpretation difficulties due to the Gravettian artefacts age and the postdepositional modifications of the analysed industry, the interpretation was made with the great care. Therefore, it is more probable that some of the tools were interpreted as unused rather than falsely being considered as used. The results proved that there could be a correlation between the type of the settlement (period/location) and working activities observed via use-wear traces on the chipped industry.

The parallel results from the LPA and HPA methods confirmed the adequacy of using them both for this assemblage as some traces would not be sufficiently detected using only one approach (see chapter 7.8). Also, the HPA method considerably helped with the interpretation of the LPA detected traces, although the microscope observation was negatively affected by the postdepositional modifications.

The interpretation of the worked materials corresponded with those reported in microwear studies of the other Palaeolithic sites, including the dominance of hide processing traces and the lack of traces originating from soft vegetables and wood. Although, these two different raw materials were extensively used in the chipped industry, except for minor minutiae, it seems that real differences did not exist in the selection of either flint or radiolarite for tool making or tool usage.

The interpreted use of the analysed tools in general corresponded with the typological etymology, i.e. the scrapers were mostly used for transversal motion, blades for longitudinal etc., although, every individual tool must be considered independently of the typological classification (see chapter 7). However, an attempt to clarify the "puzzle" concerning microliths, using the use-wear analysis has not brought any significant result (see chapter 7.6). In addition, no significant morphological differences in specific typological groups connected to different worked materials were revealed.

Finally, neither flint nor radiolarite proved to be more suitable and thus it would not be worthy to favour only one of them for microwear analysis. Both raw materials allowed for similar results and represented similar difficulties.

Fig. 3-2 Use-wear traces: ivory/antler graving, art. #27354, mag. 200x

Fig. 3-3 Use-wear traces: "polish 10", art. #23354, mag. 200x

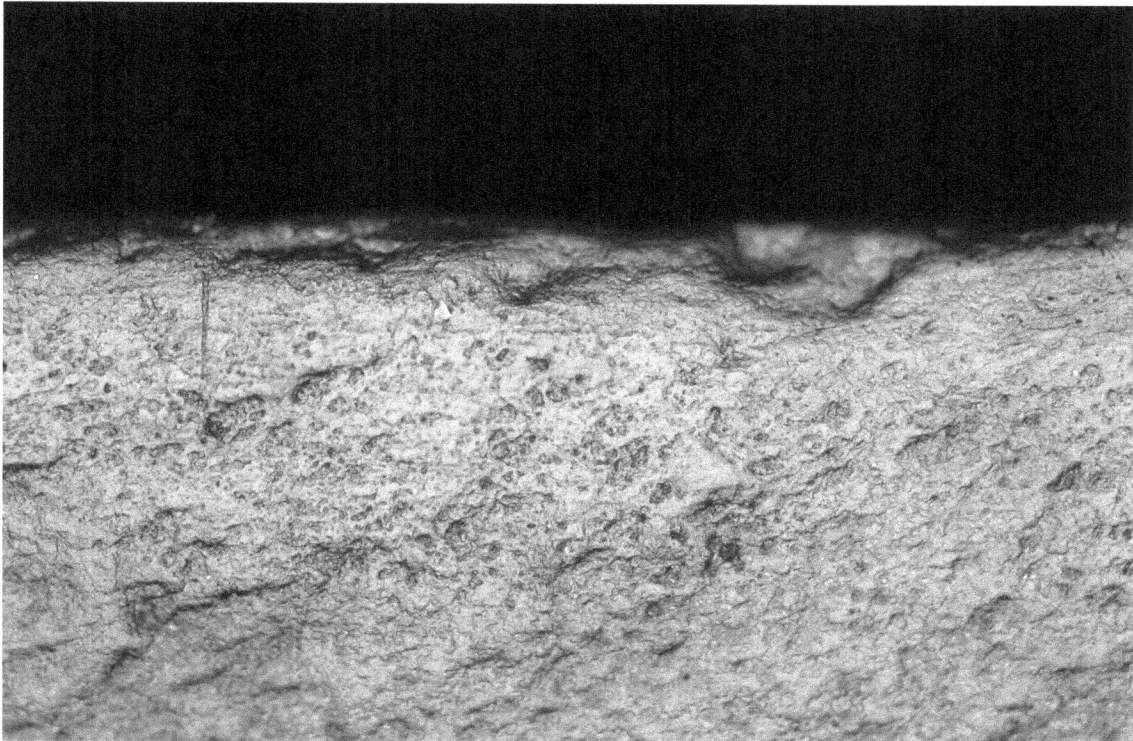

Fig. 3-4 Use-wear traces: hide cutting, art. #534457, mag. 200x

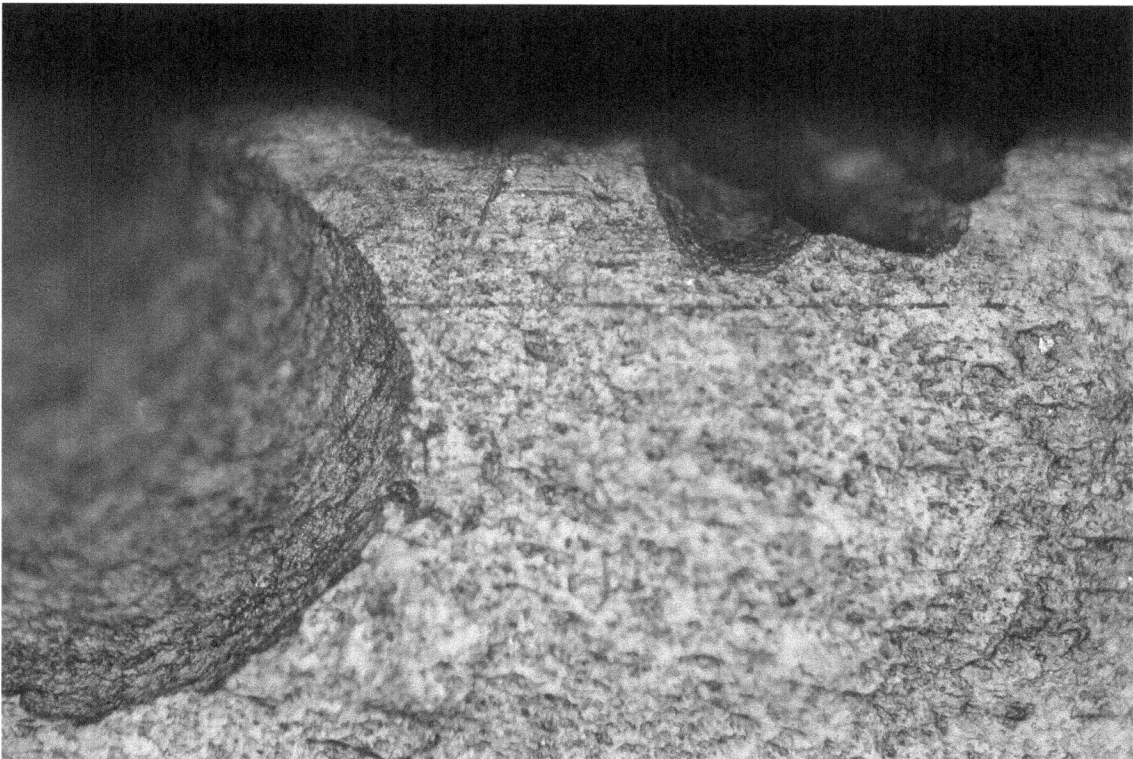

Fig. 3-5 Use-wear traces: hide cutting, art. #62971, mag. 200x

Fig. 3–6 Use-wear traces: hide scraping, art. #517957, mag. 200x

Fig. 3–7 Use-wear traces: hide scraping, art. #115771, mag. 200x

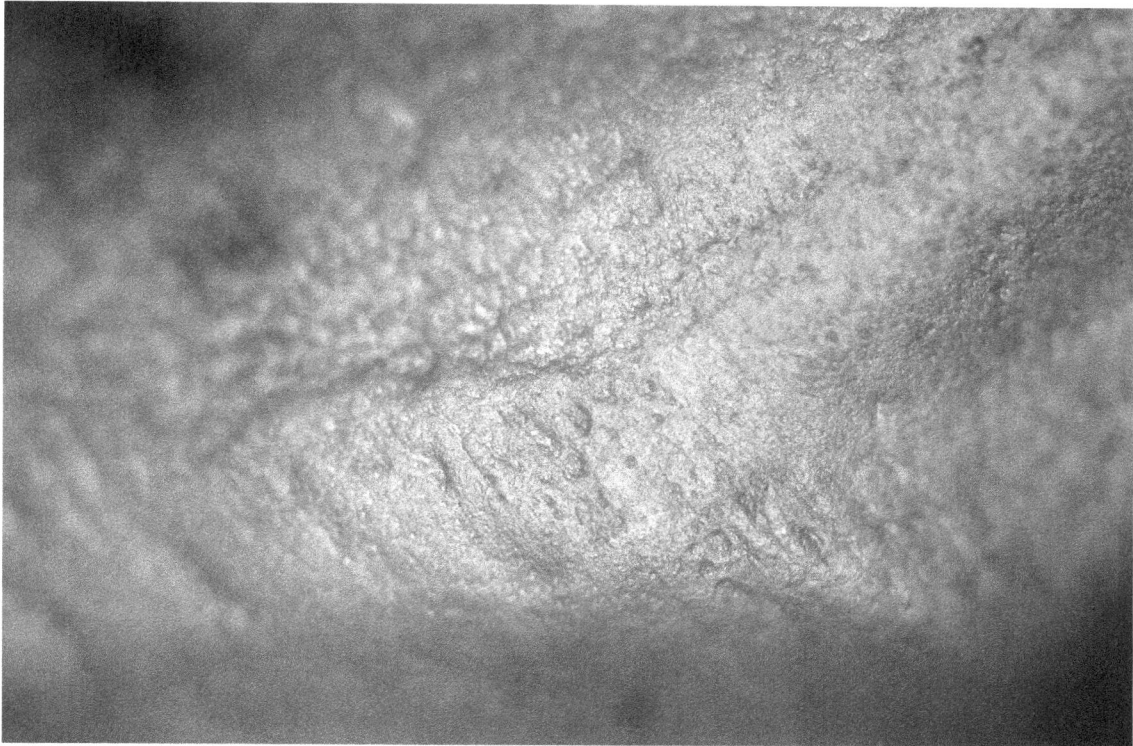

Fig. 3–8 Use-wear traces: hide scraping, art. #7670, mag. 200x

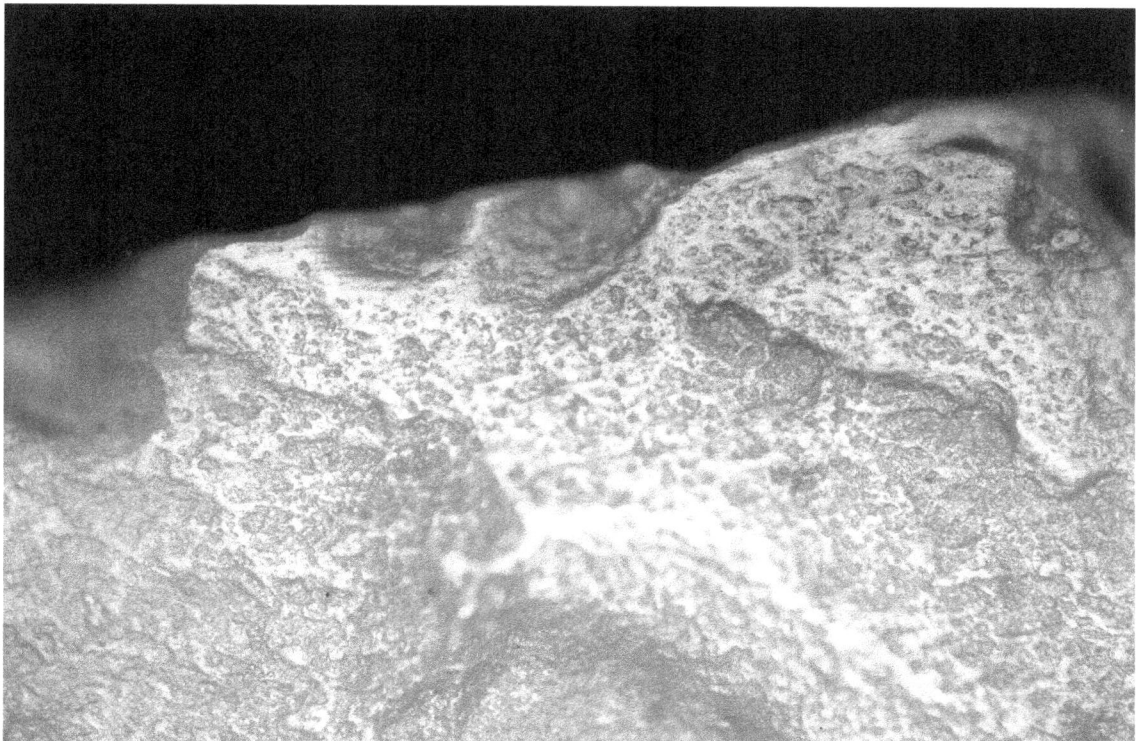

Fig. 3-9 Use-wear traces: wood cutting, art. #6270, mag. 200x

I/A

27354

I/A

27554

HI

85454

I/A

52654

I/A

27754

HI

191054

HI

139454

0   3cm

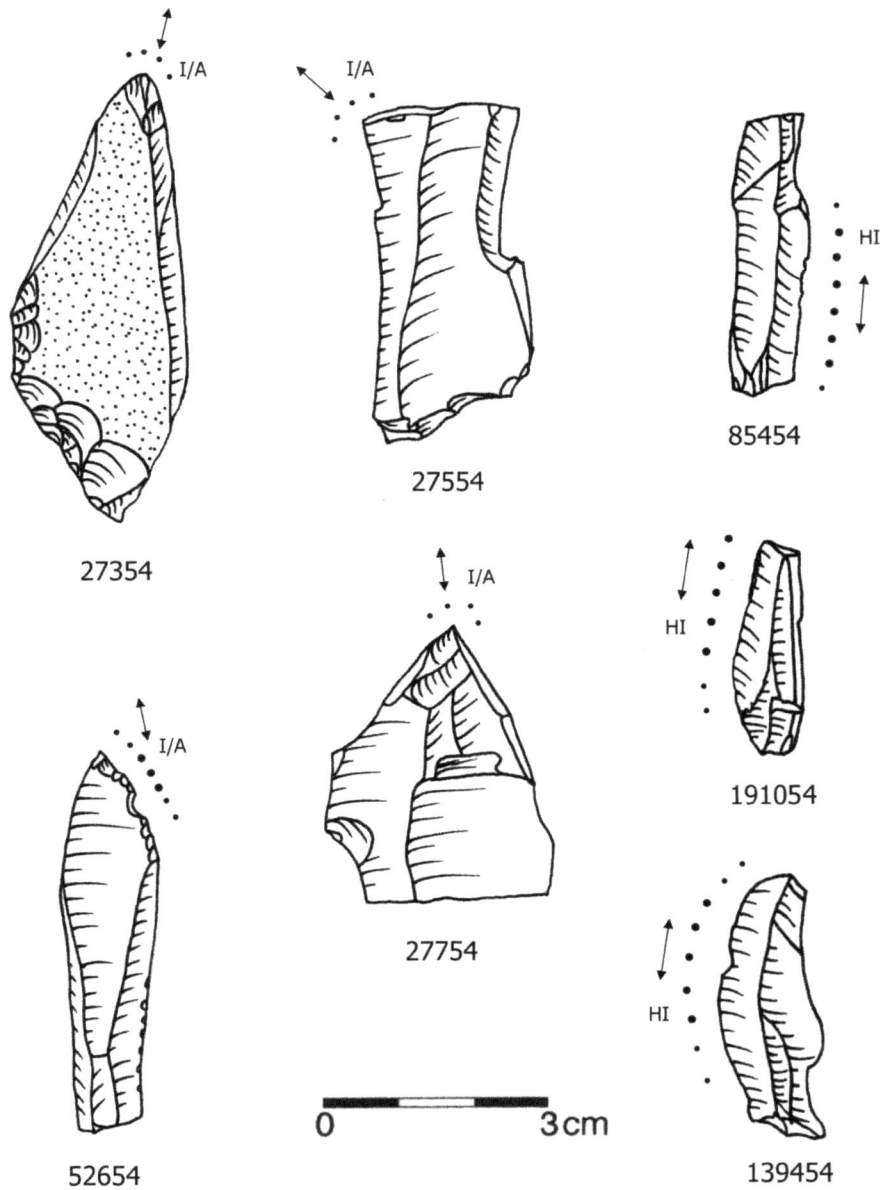

Fig. 3-10 Pavlov I 1954 (central) artefacts. The dots indicate the location and intensity of the development of the observed traces. The arrows indicate the direction of the tool motion. Worked materials: HI=hide, I/A=ivory/antler.

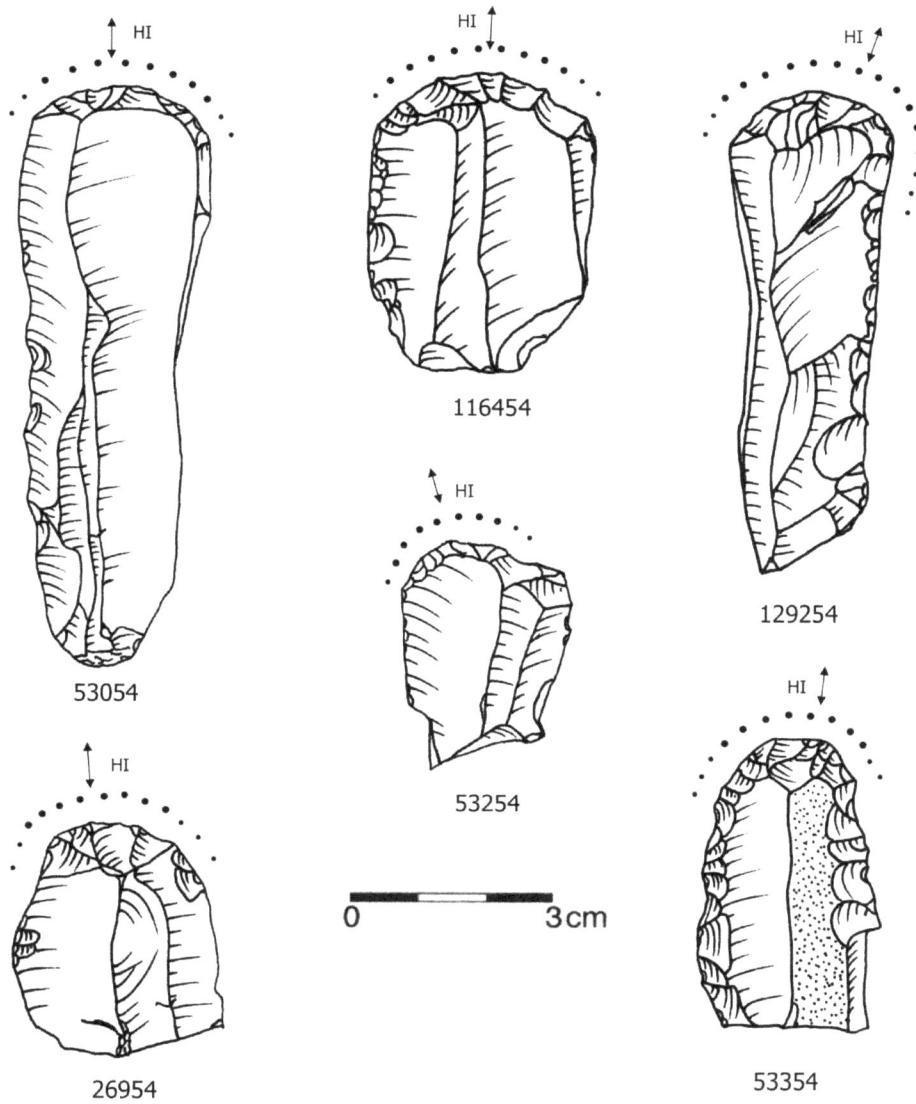

Fig. 3-11 Pavlov I 1954 (central) artefacts. The dots indicate the location and intensity of the development of the observed traces. The arrows indicate the direction of the tool motion. Worked materials: HI=hide.

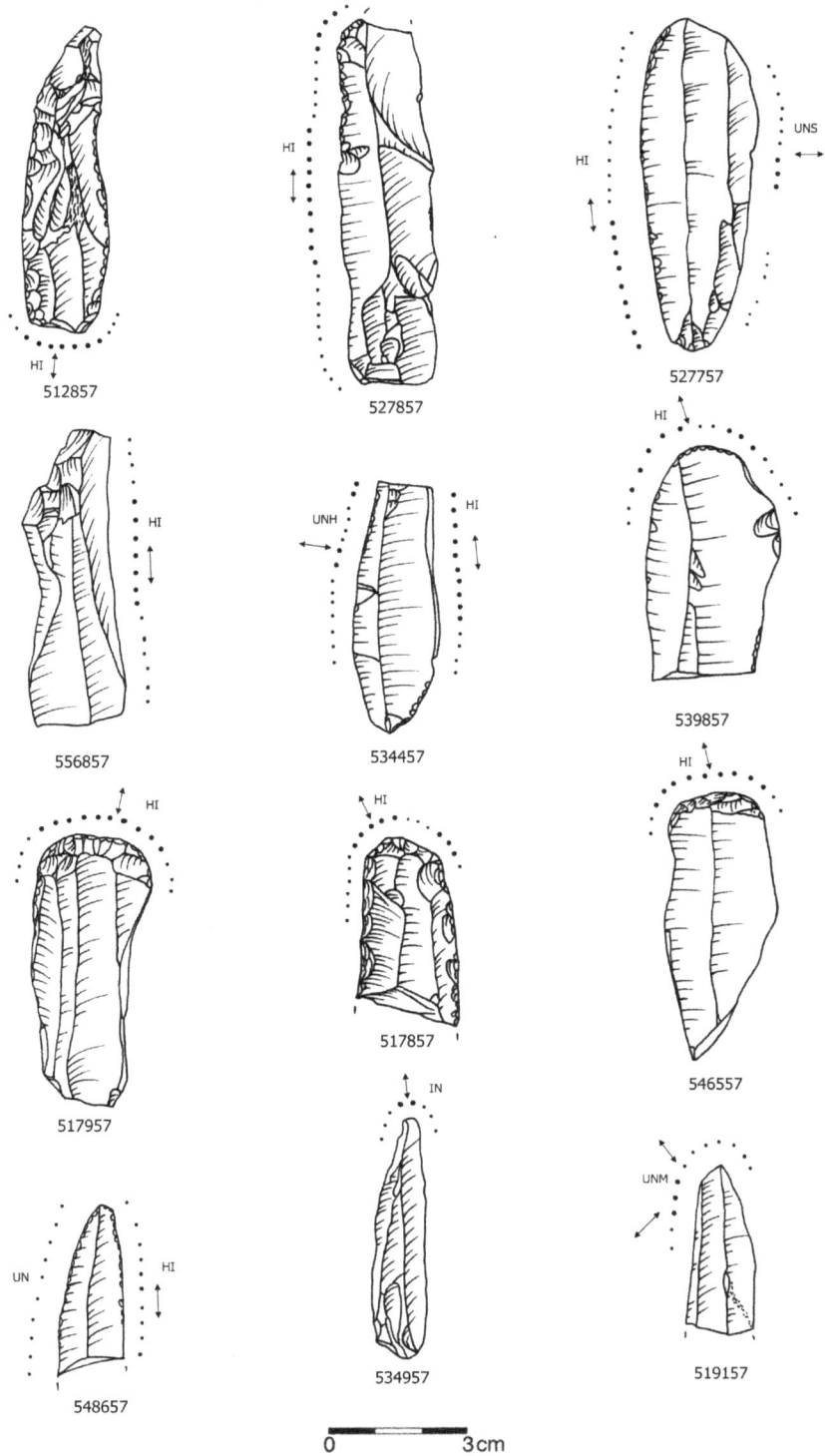

Fig. 3-12 Pavlov I 1957 (periphery) artefacts. The dots indicate the location and intensity of the development of the observed traces. The arrows indicate the direction of the tool motion. Worked materials: HI=hide, UNM=unspecified medium hard, UNS=unspecified soft, UNH=unspecified hard, IN=inorganic, UN=unspecified.

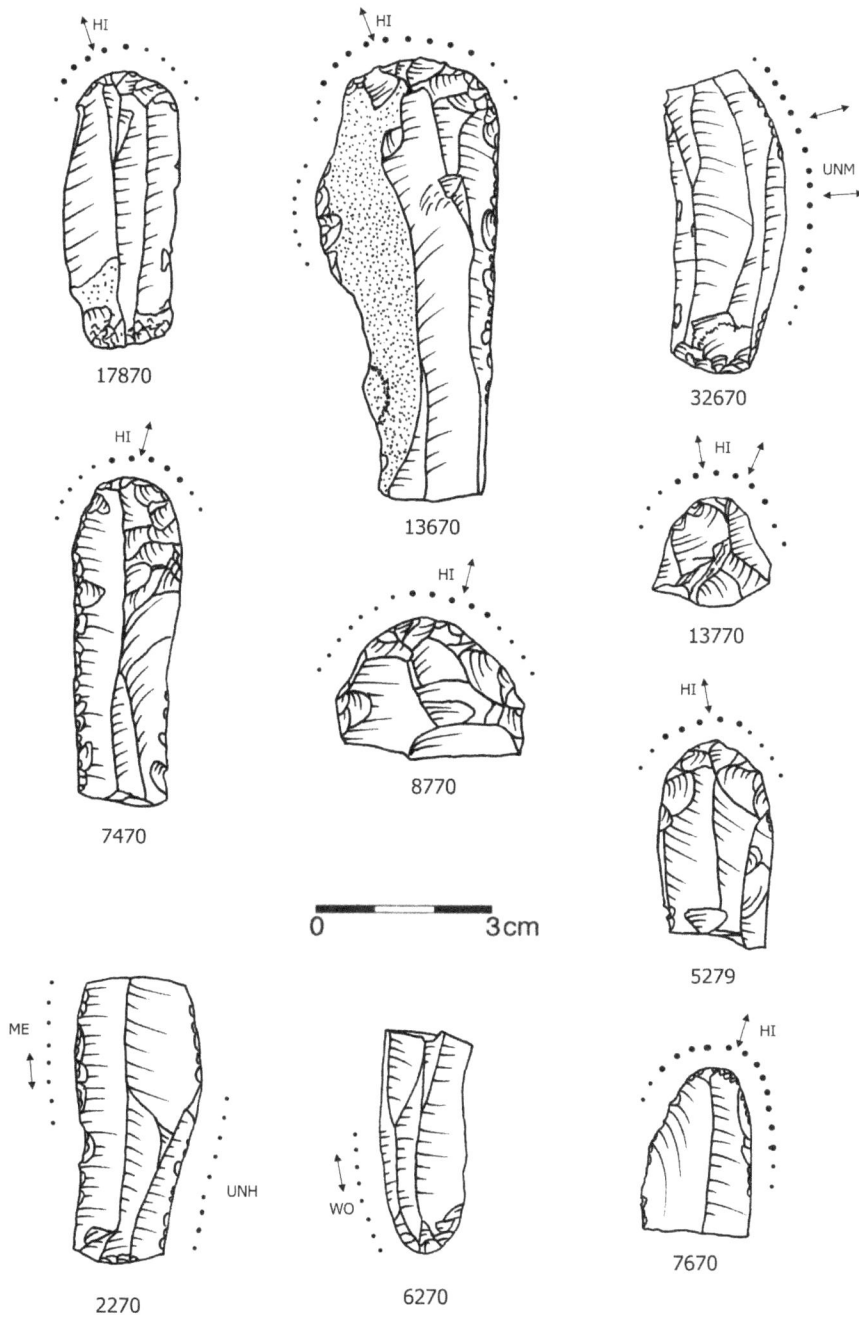

Fig. 3-13 Pavlov I 1970 (periphery) artefacts. The dots indicate the location and intensity of the development of the observed traces. The arrows indicate the direction of the tool motion. Worked materials: HI=hide, UNM=unspecified medium hard, UNH=unspecified hard, ME=meat, WO=wood.

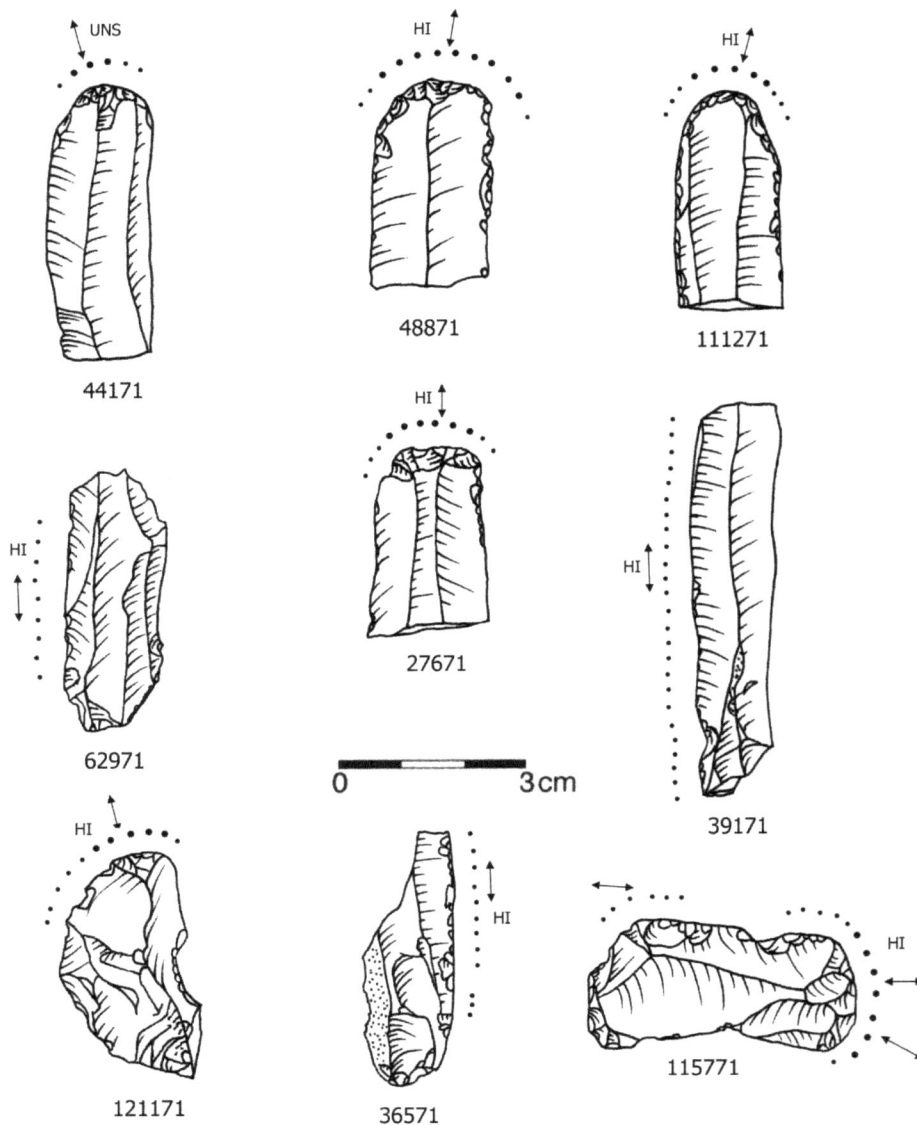

Fig. 3-14 Pavlov I 1971 (periphery) artefacts. The dots indicate the location and intensity of the development of the observed traces. The arrows indicate the direction of the tool motion. Worked materials: HI=hide, UNS=unspecified soft.

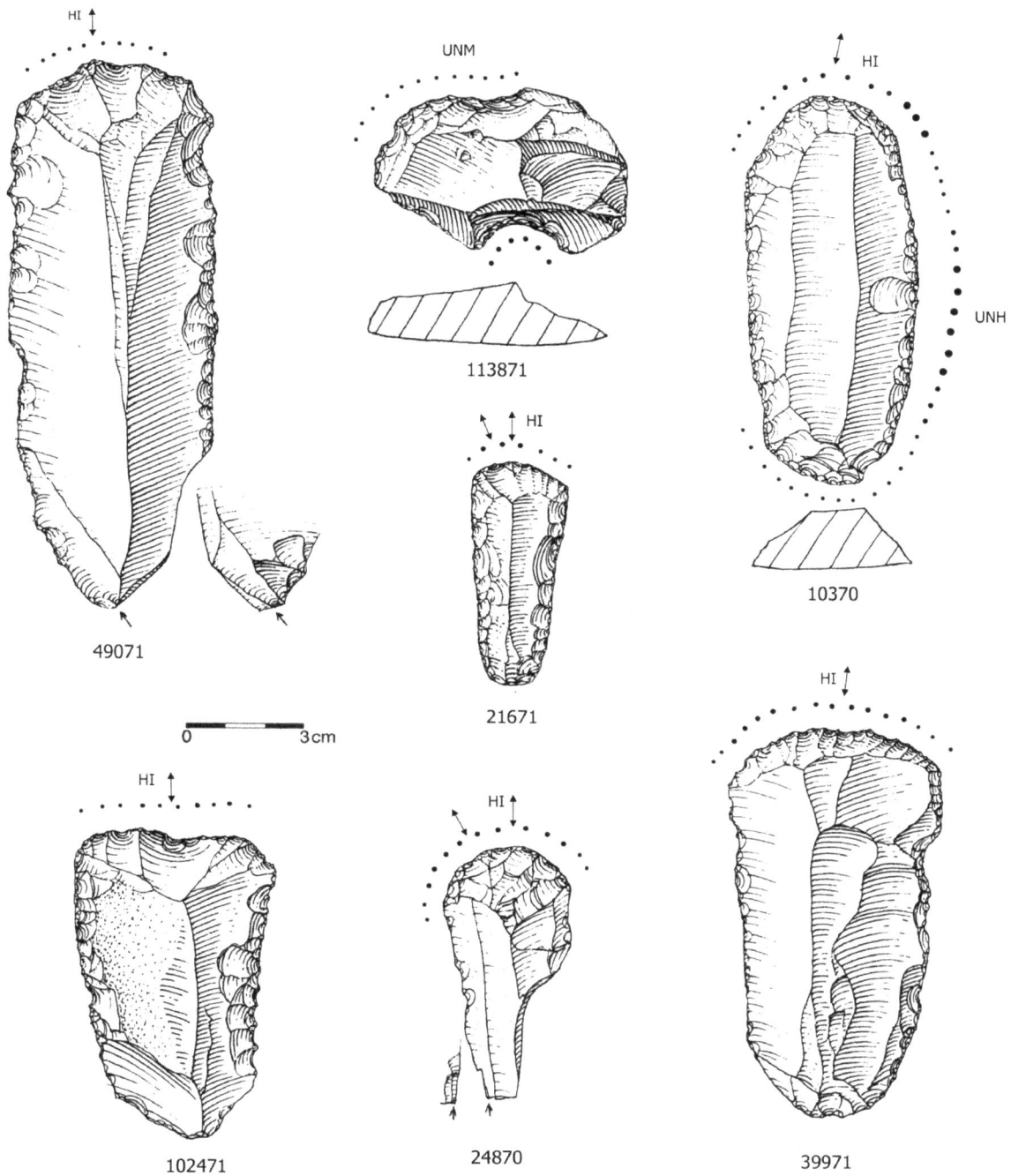

Fig. 3-15 Pavlov I 1970-71 (periphery) artefacts, drawing by B. Klíma. The dots indicate the location and intensity of the development of the observed traces. The arrows indicate the direction of the tool motion. Worked materials: HI=hide, UNM=unspecified medium hard, UNH=unspecified hard.

4. Dolní Věstonice II-A (excavation 1999)

The sites of Dolní Věstonice (I, II) are well known for the extensive Late Palaeolithic settlement (28 000 - 25 000 BP), which Karel Absolon had began to excavate in 1924. The excavations were continued by Bohuslav Klíma and then by Jiří Svoboda who directs the excavations at present. The site of Dolní Věstonice II is located on a loessic ridge just outside the village of Dolní Věstonice. It consists of several areas: the brickyard, northern and western slopes, the top area and a mammoth bone deposit.

The peripheral locality II-A on the northern slopes probably represented only short term but recurrent occupations (Svoboda 1991, Klíma 1995). This site was partially excavated in 1999 (Fig. 4-1), in order to explore the nature of the site and to protect it from further disturbance, as the stone artefacts and bones were continuously ploughed to the surface. The further fieldwork is foreseen. The research reports including the microwear analysis were published in Památky archeologické XCII/1 2001 (Šajnerová, 2001).

The assemblage was selected for the micro-wear analysis for two reasons:

- to compare the degree of the postdepositional and post-excavation modifications between the newly excavated pieces and the old excavated assemblages from Pavlov I
- to compare the results of micro-wear analysis with those from Pavlov I and inspect if they confirm differences in the type of settlement.

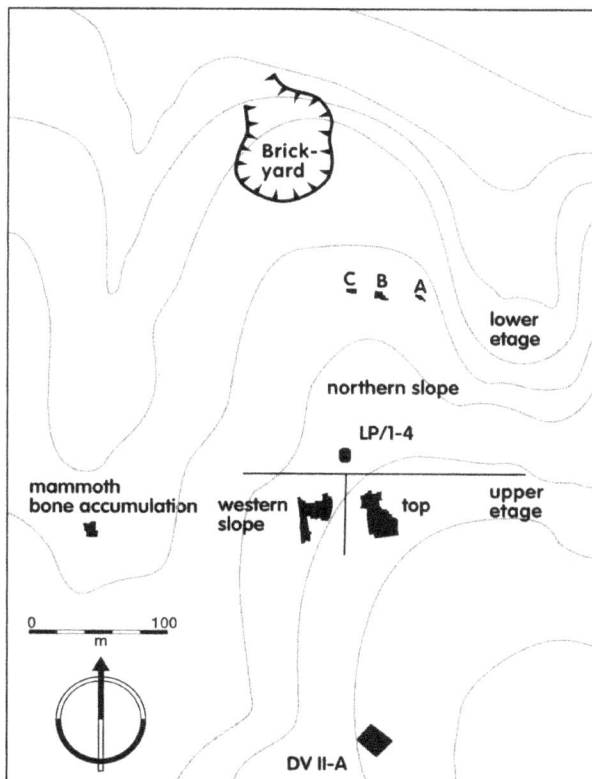

Fig. 4-1 General plan of Dolní Věstonice II and IIA excavations, by Verpoorte (2001).

4.1 Material and sampling

The Research Center for Paleolithic and Paleoethnology in Dolní Věstonice, the Institute of Archaeology ASCR in Brno, provided a total of 92 pieces of chipped industry originating from the excavation of the site DV IIA 1999, from the intact drills A and B, which were not affected with ploughing.

The artefacts were further pre-selected prior to the detailed microanalysis. The pre-selection was made by following criteria connected with the probability of the possible usage of the artefact. The criteria were based on

those used by other analysts (e.g. Gijn 1990; Juel Jensen and Petersen 1995):

- retouch size < 1 mm (i.e. "use-retouch", mostly connected with the tool use)
- retouch size of 1 mm or bigger (intentional retouch)
- naked eye visible polish
- straight edge (length at least 1 cm)
- protruding point

Thus, a total of 41 artefacts (flint 91%, radiolarite 7%, unknown 2%) were chosen for the microanalysis. The detailed distribution of the raw materials and typological groups is presented in Tab. 4-1. The retouched pieces made up 12% of the analysed implements.

Tab. 4-1 Distribution of the typological groups and the raw materials.

Typology group	Flint	Radiolarite	Unknown	Total
Blades	22	0	1	23
Flakes	13	1	0	14
Burins	0	1	0	1
Microliths	2	1	0	3
Total count	37	3	1	41

4.2 Results and discussion

The analysis was performed in the Laboratory for restoration of archaeological metal artefacts in the Archaeological Institute ASCR in Prague, employing the metallographic microscope Olympus. Unfortunately, its configuration was not fully suitable for microwear analysis and it was not equipped with the low working distance objectives, which are necessary for focusing on the rough and oblique surface of the stone artefacts. Therefore, the available magnification used for most of the observation was only 100x. The higher magnification (200x) allowed for observation of only small parts of the focused surface with a shallow depth of acuity that did not permit recognition of the polish attributes necessary for the interpretation of the contact material. Thus, it is possible that some weakly developed traces were missed or misinterpreted as postdepositional modifications.

Tab. 4-2 Degree of the interpreted use-wear traces plus a composition of the retouched pieces in the analysed sample.

Use-wear traces	
Not interpretable	12% (5%)
Interpretable traces	27% (12%)
No traces	61% (83%)
Retouched pieces	12% (5%)
% of used retouched pieces	40%

Notes:
 x% - values of the analysed sample
(x%) - recalculated values for the primary sample

From the pre-selected sample, 25 pieces from 41 analysed implements showed no use-wear traces, which made up about 62%; recalculated for the whole sample it makes up over 80% (Tab. 4-2). However, the whole sample might not represent a complete assemblage due to the extension of the trenches and the collection of the surface artefacts (Svoboda, pers. comm.). The entire assemblage was affected by white patina, which contributed to the lower interpretability of the analysis. Due to postdepositional modifications, 5 pieces had wear traces completely uninterpretable by both the LPA and HPA methods. Interpretable signs of use-wear were traced on 11 pieces (Tab. 4-2). The second most frequent postdepositional modification was bright spots (friction gloss). Similarly

to Pavlov I, black residual spots of an unknown (most probably of postdepositional) origin were quite frequent (Fig. 4-2).

The Dolní Věstonice 1999 excavation was considered to be a short term settlement and the low percentage of used tools could correspond with that; however, see the full discussion of the correlation of the proportion of used tools and the type of settlement in chapter 7.7. Although the results of a short term settlement may resemble the results of the Pavlov periphery samples (see the previous chapter, Tab. 3-3), the typological structure (e.g. there were no scrapers excavated in Dolní Věstonice in 1999) and the degree of development of the use-wear traces were different (Tab. 4-3). The most significant difference was the lack of extensively used tools (cf. Pavlov I, Tab. 3-4).

Tab. 4-3 Degree of development of the interpreted use-wear traces.

Degree of traces	
Unsure/possible use	55%
Light use	18%
Medium use	27%
Extensive use	0%

Some of the examined artefacts could have had more than one used area or could have been retooled – the rest of the originally used areas could still be visible. With the exception of one artefact with two interpreted AUAs (9%), the used artefacts displayed only one actually used area (AUA). This result greatly differs to the Pavlov I findings where supernumeral AUAs appeared on 25% of the used tools excavated in the central area and about 13% of the used tools excavated in the peripheral areas (see the previous chapter).

The distribution of the tool fragments in the analysed samples was almost equal, the complete, distal and proximal fragments made up about one third each. However, the traces were observed more often on the distal and proximal fragments than on the complete tools (Tab. 4-4).

Tab. 4-4 Distribution of the tool fragments and the location of the use-wear traces.

Fragment	% of the analysed sample	% of used fragments
Complete	38%	38%
Distal	24%	50%
Medial	5%	0%
Proximal	21%	56%
Unsure	12%	20%

The overview of the interpreted traces categorised by the hardness of the worked material (LPA) is presented in Tab. 4-5. The overview of the interpreted traces using the HPA method is presented in Tab. 4-6. Likewise in the Pavlov I assemblage, the soft materials were the most frequently worked items (Tab. 4-5). However, the prevalent worked material was soft animal tissues (Tab. 4-6), unlike hide in the Pavlov I settlement (over 50% AUAs, see Tab. 3-8 and Tab. 3-9). Hide processing was probably a minor activity and together with the dominance of the soft animal tissue traces, the results correspond with an anticipated short term settlement.

The direction of the tool motion during use was interpreted according to the direction of the microscars, polish and striations. The most frequent working motion was longitudinal (Tab. 4-7), in accordance to the percentage representation of blades in the assemblage (56% of the analysed sample).

Tab. 4-5 Interpretation of the use-wear traces using a binocular microscope (LPA).

Typology group	Hard material	Soft material	Unsure	Total AUAs	No traces (pieces)
Blades	2	5	6	13	11
Flakes	1	1		2	12
Burins				0	1
Microliths		1		1	2
Total count	3	7	6	16	26
% of total AUAs	19%	44%	37%		
Total % of analysed pieces	7%	17%	15%		63%

Tab. 4-6 Interpretation of the worked materials using an incident light microscope (HPA).

Typology group	Antler/ wood	Hide	Soft animal	Unsure	Total AUAs	No traces (pieces)
Flakes	1	1			2	12
Blades	2	1	4	5	12	12
Microliths			1		1	2
Burins					0	1
Total count	3	2	5	5	15	27
% of total AUAs	20%	14%	33%	33%		
Total % of analysed pieces	7%	5%	11%	11%		66%

Tab. 4-7 Interpretation of the working motions.

Typology group	Boring	Diagonal	Longitudinal	Transversal	Hafting	Unsure	Total AUAs	No traces (pieces)
Flakes	1			1			2	12
Blades		1	5	1	3	2	12	12
Microliths		1					1	
Burins			1				1	2
Total count	1	2	6	2	3	2	16	26
% of total AUAs	6%	12,5%	37,5%	12,5%	19%	12,5%		
Total % of analysed pieces	2%	5%	15%	5%	7%	5%		63%

4.3 Conclusion

The analysed sample exposed a low percentage of used implements (about 12% or 17%, including the uninterpretable pieces), which may correspond with the low number of intentionally retouched tools (only 5 pieces). Similar results were also noticed by S. Tomášková (1991) in her analysis of the assemblage from the Dolní Věstonice II – Western slope excavation where only 2,5% of the analysed tools displayed use-wear traces. However, the postdepositional modifications and the old age of the artefacts may have caused a reduction of use-wear traces that were preserved on the surface. The interpretation was limited by the inadequate microscope objectives, which had low working distance.

Therefore, it is possible that some lightly used tools were interpreted as unused.

The results proved a possible correlation between the settlement period/location and the working activities, observed as use-wear traces on the chipped industry. Considering the prevalence of traces interpreted as the cutting of soft animal tissue, the excavated site seems to have rather been used as a place for short term working activities or occasional tool manufacture. The same conclusion was previously suggested by Svoboda (1991) or Klíma (1995), as well as Tomášková (1991).

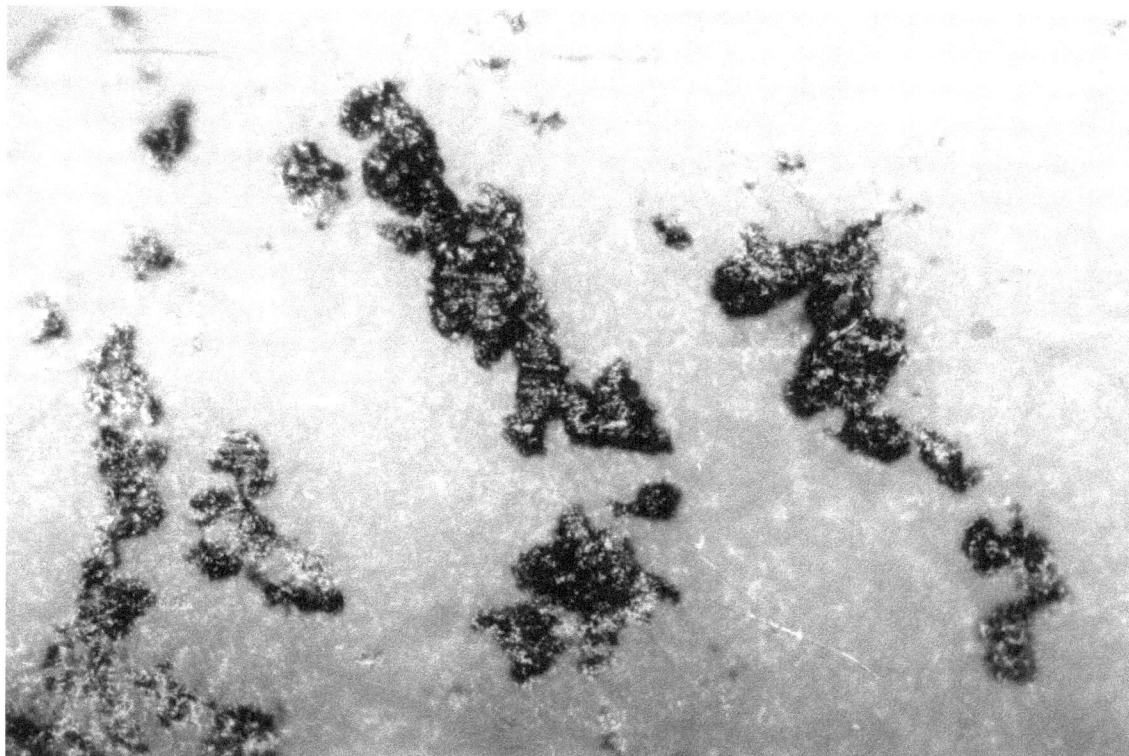

Fig. 4-2 Residual spots with postdepositional striations, art.# 2999 (200x).

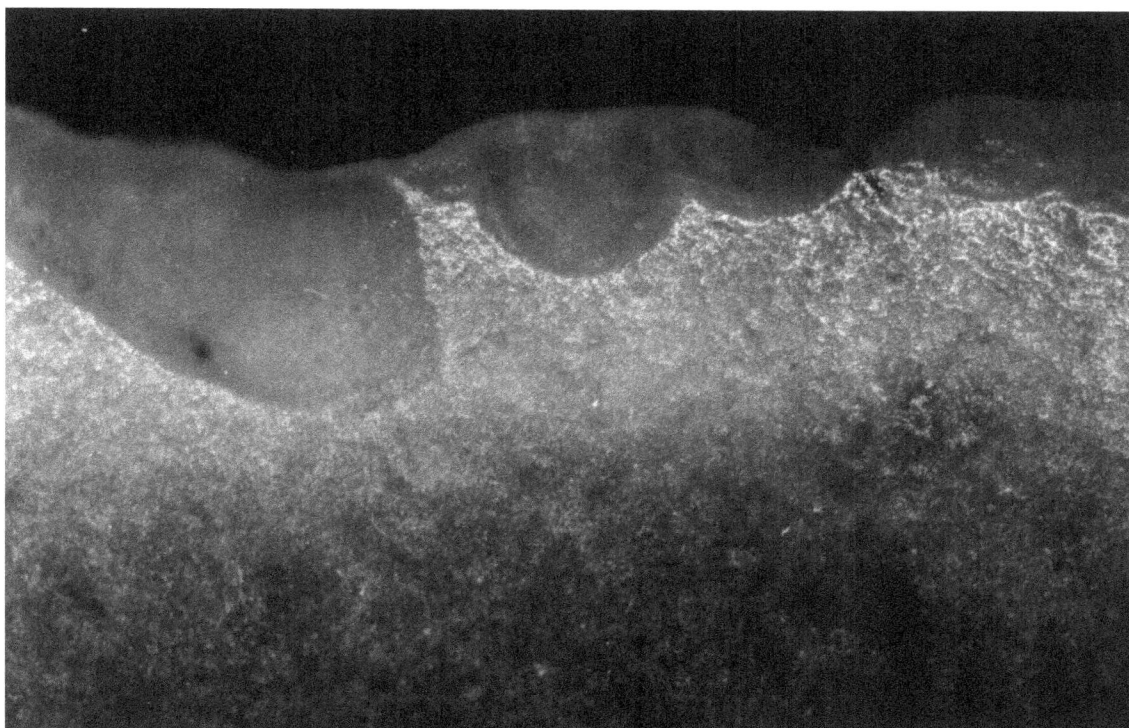

Fig. 4-3 Polish and scars with diagonal orientation art.# 2299 (100x).

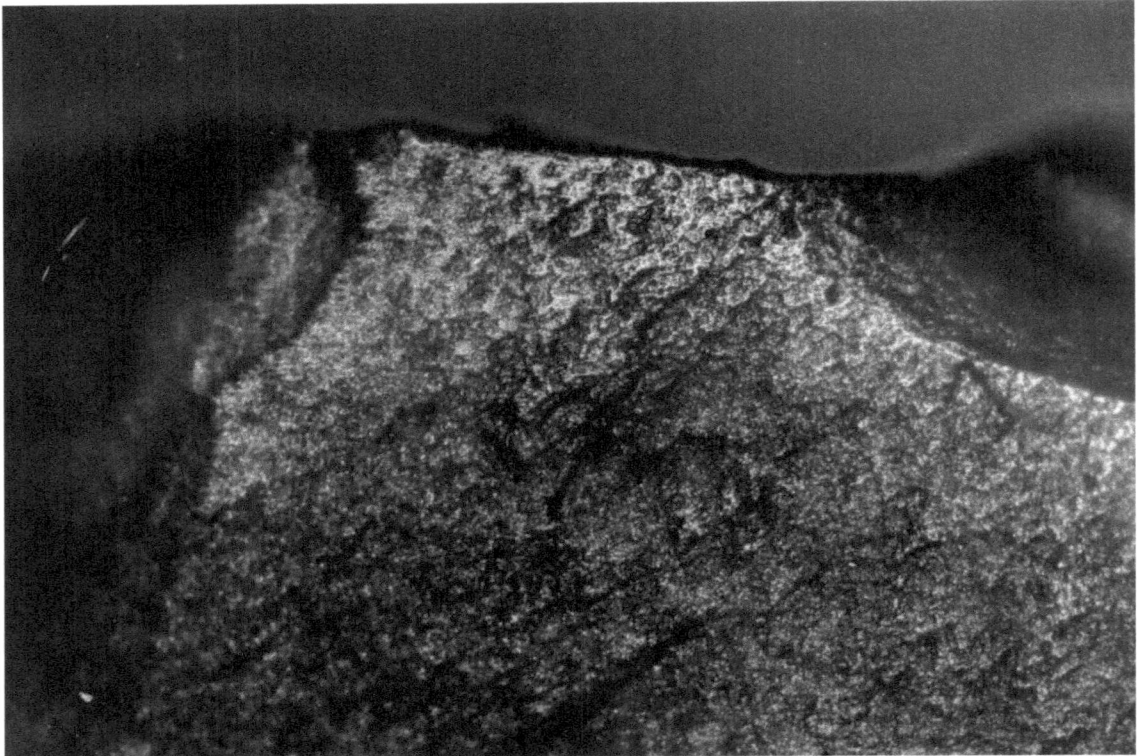

Fig. 4-4 Polish with a distinct parallel orientation along the edge, interpreted as cutting of hard material, antler or hard wood, art.# 2299 (100x).

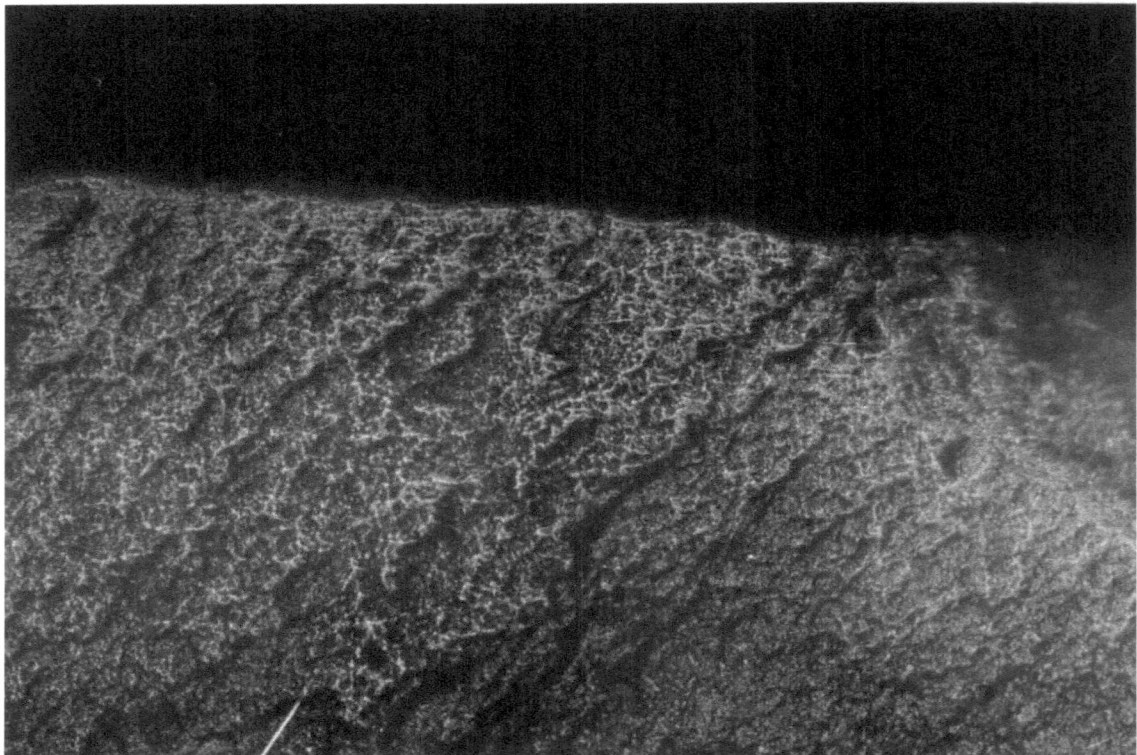

Fig. 4-5 The same position as Fig.4-4, art.# 2299 (200x).

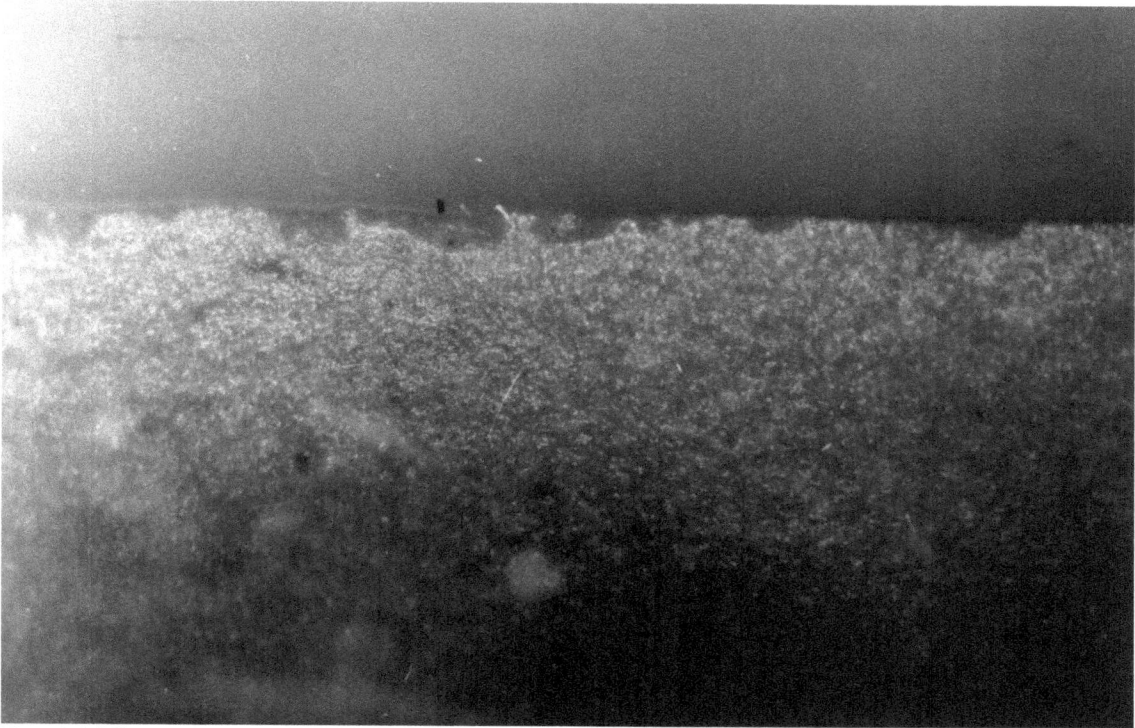

Fig. 4-6 "Greasy lustre" polish together with diagonal scars interpreted as cutting of soft animal material, art.# 2399 (100x).

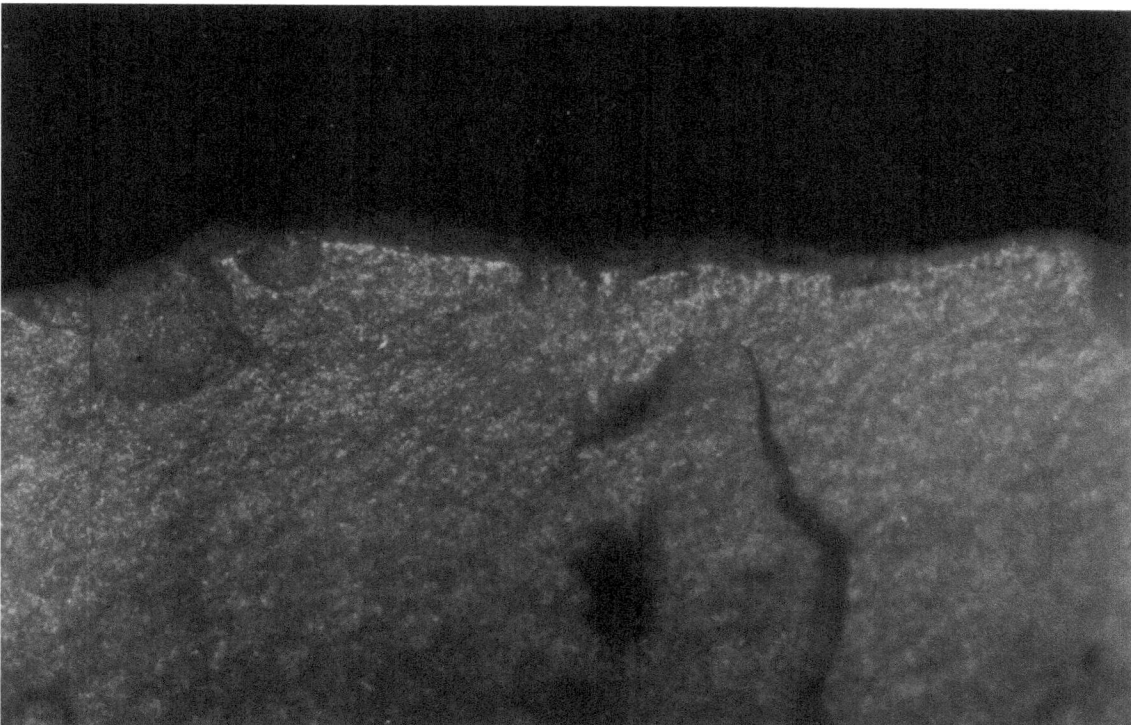

Fig. 4-7 Perpendicularly oriented polish with perpendicular scars and edge rounding interpreted as scraping of soft material (probably hide) art.# 3199 (100x).

5. Stránská Skála III

The site of Stránská skála lies 310 m above sea level in the Brno basin and covers an area approximately 1,500 m long and 400 m wide. The sediments and Jurassic outcrops have attracted scientific attention since 1881. The faunal assemblage from the Lower/Middle Palaeolithic was discovered at the beginning of the twentieth century in the small caves on the western slope and its systematic multidisciplinary excavations were conducted by R. Musil (1956-72) and K. Valoch (1997-98) (Svoboda and Valoch 2003).

The Upper Palaeolithic settlement at Stránská skála covers two main occupation stages, the Bohunician (about 35 - 40 000 P.B.) and the Aurignacian (33 - 30 000 B.P.). The site is situated near the top of the Stránská skála bedrock and was excavated from 1982 to 1999 (Fig. 5-1). Unfortunately, due to loess sediments and paleosols

chemistry the archaeological material was restricted to lithics; in addition the site itself is supplied by rich local chert outcrops. Thus, the archaeological evaluation focused mostly on the raw material, lithic distribution patterns at the sites, technology, typology and use-wear analysis (Svoboda and Bar-Yosef 2003). The final monograph "Stránská skála: Origins of Upper Palaeolithic in the Brno basin, Moravia, Czech Republic" including the microwear analysis was published in Dolnověstonické studie 10 (Šajnerová 2003a).

The first attempt for microwear analysis was made by J. Svoboda (1987) on 3 selected artefacts (sidescraper, bec and borer) using the electron microscope to observe in more details the macroscopically visible signs of use on the use-damaged edges.

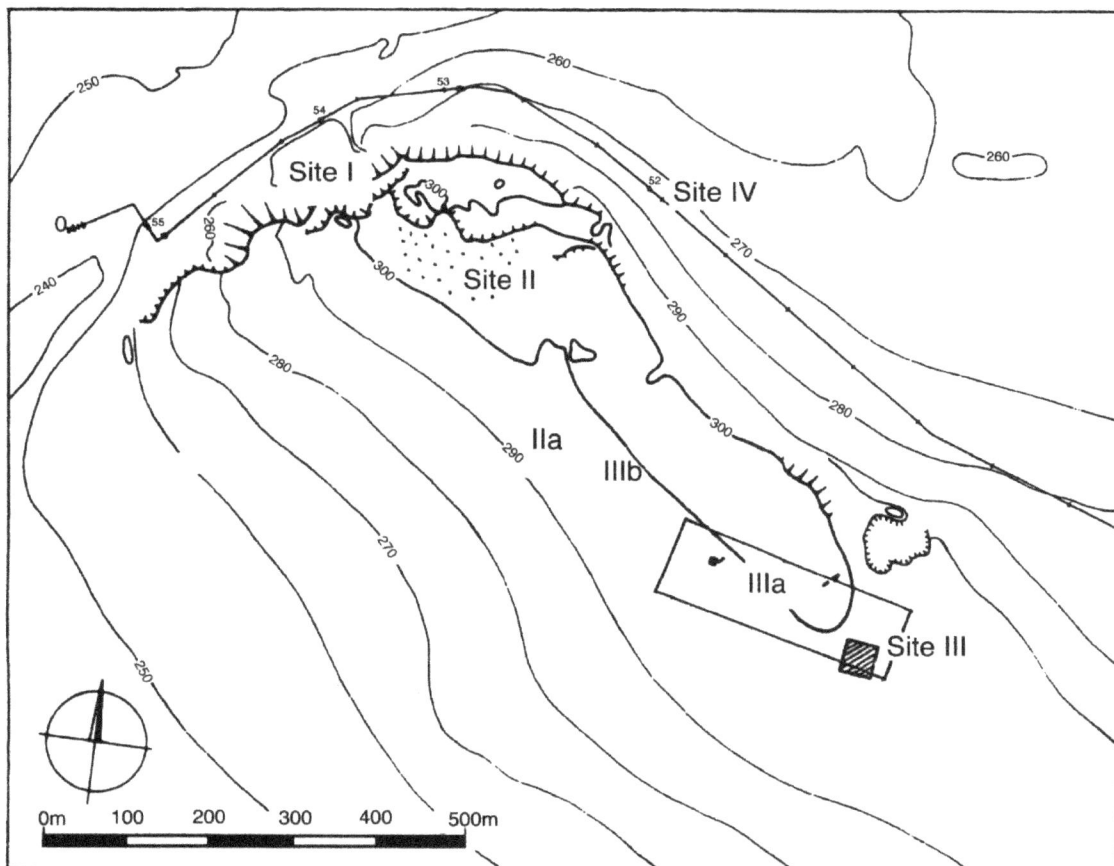

Fig. 5-1 Plan of the Stránská skála excavations, after J. Svoboda (2000).

5.1 Material and sampling

Stránská skála was one of the important sites during the period of early settlement of Moravia. Unfortunately, the preliminary research of the assemblage showed a high level of patination. Therefore, only small samples from the major typological groups were chosen for use-wear analysis to roughly extend the comprehension of the activities performed at this important site. The selection of the samples for use-wear analysis was made by J. Svoboda (Research Center for Paleolithic and Paleoethnology in Dolní Věstonice, Institute of Archaeology ASCR in Brno), based on the main typological groups that were most likely to have positive microwear results. The artefacts with macroscopic traces of use were preferably selected.

The total amount of analysed implements from Stránská skála was 42 pieces. Two Bohunician samples were selected: 14 pieces from Stránská skála III (1982) and 27 pieces from Stránská skála IIIa (1984). Furthermore, one massive Aurignacian endscraper from the upper layer of site IIIa (1984) was analysed for comparative purposes. The raw materials varied; from Stránská skála (SS) chert (83%) to the less frequent Krumlovský Les (KL) chert (10%) and radiolarite (7%) (Tab. 5-1).

The detailed typological and raw material description of the selected samples:

- 14 pieces from Stránská skála III, 1982. Typologically, the sample consists of 5 Levallois points, 6 endscrapers, 2 sidescrapers and 1 bec. From the viewpoint of raw materials, 7 pieces of Stránská skála chert (SS chert), 4 pieces of Krumlovský Les chert (KL chert) and 3 pieces of radiolarite were represented.

- 27 pieces from Stránská skála IIIa, 1984. Typologically, the sample consists of 5 Levallois points (in one case with endscraper on Levallois point), 1 ventroterminal point, 5 endscrapers (one of them thick), 5 sidescrapers and retouched flakes, 2 truncated blades and 9 notches and denticulates. All are made of the Stránská skála chert.

- One massive Aurignacian endscraper (Stránská skála chert) from the upper layer of site IIIa, 1984, was analysed for comparative purposes.

Tab. 5-1 Distribution of the typological groups and the raw materials.

Typology group	SS Chert	KL Chert	Radiolarite	Total
Truncated blades	2			2
Notches	9			9
Points	10			10
Endscrapers	9	3	1	13
Sidescrapers	5	1	1	7
Bec			1	1
Total count	35	4	3	42

5.2 Results and discussion

Use-wear analysis was carried out on a very small sample of implements only to demonstrate the possibilities of use-wear analysis at this site. Trace interpretation was based both on the LPA and HPA methods. From 42 analysed implements 12 pieces showed no use-wear traces which is 29%, further 11 pieces (26%) had wear traces undetermined using the HPA method but with an approximate determination of hardness using the LPA method, and finally 19 pieces (45%) showed clear signs of use-wear using the HPA method (Tab. 5-3). The results concerning the amounts of used and unused pieces are useful only for orientation purposes and cannot be compared with other researches due to the sampling method (Tab. 5-2). The samples only pinpointed the

major types of tools and, in a complex view, they were not representative of the whole assemblage.

Tab. 5-2 Degree of the interpreted use-wear traces plus a composition of the retouched pieces in the analysed samples.

Interpreted traces	
Not interpretable	0%
Interpretable traces	71%
No traces	29%
Retouched pieces	90%
% of used retouched pieces	24%

Generally, most of the flint artefacts show moderate to heavy white patination and postdepositional sheen which decreased the possibility of interpretation using an incident light microscope. It was often ascertained that one side was more patinated than the other. In a few cases the ventral side looked almost fresh. However, there was no significant difference between patination on the dorsal and ventral side, the distribution was random.

Tab. 5-3 Degree of development of the interpreted use-wear traces.

Degree of traces	
Unsure/possible use	30%
Light use	27%
Medium use	33%
Extensive use	9%

Some of the examined artefacts could have had more than one used area or could have been retooled and the rest of the originally used areas could still be visible. In 3 instances two AUAs were interpreted. One case of the supernumerary AUA was a truncated blade with both edges used, the other two cases (scrapers) displayed unsure traces that may have originated from hafting.

Tab. 5-4 Distribution of the tool fragments and the location of the use-wear traces.

Fragment	% of analysed sample	% of used fragments
Complete	73%	67%
Distal	20%	89%
Medial	4%	100%
Proximal	0%	
Unsure	2%	100%

The distribution of the tool fragments in the analysed samples was very unequal due to the specific sampling, the complete tools made up over 70%, distal parts represented 20% and proximal fragments were not present in the sample. However, the traces were observed more often on the fragments than on the complete tools (Tab.5-4). This could have been influenced by the fact that unused points made up a significant part of the complete tools.

The overview of the interpreted traces using the LPA method is presented in Tab. 5-5, the interpretation according to the HPA method follows in Tab. 5-6. The prevalent worked material was hide, which comprised about 36% of the analysed pieces. The analysis showed a clear connection between endscrapers and hide-working, but such a narrow material/activity relation was not apparent for the sidescrapers. In addition, endscrapers had the most significant interpretation of use – the only case interpreted as unsure contact material was a supernumeral AUA, probably hafting. On the contrary, sidescrapers were more frequently interpreted as being used on hard or unsure material. The point category shows a very high percentage of (probably) unused tools (70-80% of the analysed points have no traces of use).

The direction of the tool motion during its use was interpreted according to the direction of microscars and/or polish and striations. The description of the direction s related to the used edge and the results are presented in Tab. 5-7. The most frequent direction of use was the transversal motion (42%), probably due to predominance of scrapers (47%) in the sample. The second most frequent motion was longitudinal (20%).

The relation between the angle of the worked edge and the tool typology is presented in Tab. 5-8. Points had a very uniform edge angle (31°-38°) as did endscrapers (57°-89°). In contrast, the sidescrapers had a very wide range of angles of the used edges (24°-102°). The average angle of the endscraper edge was 71° and the sidescraper edge was about 58°. The results do not reveal any significant correlation between the used raw material and the edge angle (i.e. tool morphology).

Tab. 5-5 Interpretation of the use-wear traces using a binocular microscope (LPA).

Typology group	Hard material	Soft material	Unsure	Total AUAs	No traces (pieces)
Truncated blades		2		2	1
Notches	3		3	6	3
Points		2	1	3	7
Endscrapers	1	2	11	14	
Sidescrapers	2	1	4	7	1
Bec		1		1	
Total count	6	8	19	33	12
% of total AUAs	18%	24%	58%		
Total % of analysed pieces	14%	19%	45%		29%

Tab. 5-6 Interpretation of the worked materials using an incident light microscope (HPA).

Typology group	Unspec. hard	Hide	Soft animal	Minerals / soil	Unsure	Total AUAs	No traces (pieces)
Truncated blades			2			2	1
Notches		1	1		3	5	4
Points				1	1	2	8
Endscrapers	1	12			1	14	
Sidescrapers		2			4	6	2
Bec					1	1	
Total count	1	15	3	1	10	30	15
% of total AUAs	3%	50%	10%	3%	33%		
Total % of analysed pieces	2%	36%	7%	2%	24%		36%

Tab. 5-7 Interpretation of the working motions.

Typology group	Boring	Diagonal	Longitudinal	Transversal	Dynamic activities	Hafting	Unsure	Total AUAs	No traces (pieces)
Truncated blades			2					2	1
Notches		1	3	2				6	3
Points			2		1			3	7
Endscrapers				13		1		14	
Sidescrapers			2	4			1	7	1
Bec	1							1	
Total count	1	1	9	19	1	1	1	33	12
% of total AUAs	3%	3%	27%	58%	3%	3%	3%		
Total % of analysed pieces	2%	5%	15%	5%		7%	5%		63%

Tab. 5-8 Angle of the worked edges (all samples).

Typology group	0-30°	31°-60°	61°-90°	> 90°
Truncated blades		2/-/-[a]		
Notches	1/-/-	4/-/-	1/-/-	
Points		3/-/-		
Endscrapers[b]		2/1/-	7/2/1	
Sidescrapers	-/-/1	1/1/-	2/-/1	1/-/-
Bec		-/-/1		
Total count	1/-/1	12/2/1	10/2/2	1/-/-

[a] Amounts of tools made from SS chert/ KL chert/ radiolarite
[b] The angle of the hafted edge was not included.

5.3 Conclusion

The analysis showed that the use of the HPA method is an effective aid for the interpretation of the tools function even though its utilisation for the early Upper Palaeolithic artefacts is more limited than for assemblages from younger periods. The analysis was limited by the extreme white patina but this was more caused by the local climatic condition than the high age of the artefacts. Hide, accordingly to other studies of Palaeolithic assemblages, was interpreted as the predominant worked material, probably as its use-wear traces have the longest endurance against the postdepositional impact (Plisson and Mauger 1988). However, hide quite often leaves no or very little edge damage which could be observed with the LPA method. But the edge rounding, striation and polish can be detectable using the HPA method, making it quite advantageous. The hard or medium hard worked materials lend themselves a better interpretation using the LPA method than HPA; therefore the hard contact materials can be interpreted only approximately.

Use-wear traces were most frequently observed on endscrapers and sidescrapers. Interpretation of notches and truncated blades was based more on the LPA method. The sample is too small to permit a more complete interpretation of the lack of discernable traces, especially on pointed flakes. The high percentage of unused points could be caused by the fact that most of them have blunt and imperfect tips, i.e. these points appeared to have been knapped improperly. From this perspective, most of them could have been waste products. The recycling of the points as butchering tools was not confirmed (cf. Kay 1996).

Fig. 5-2 Use-wear polish: hide scraping, ventral side art. #1219-32/82, (200x).

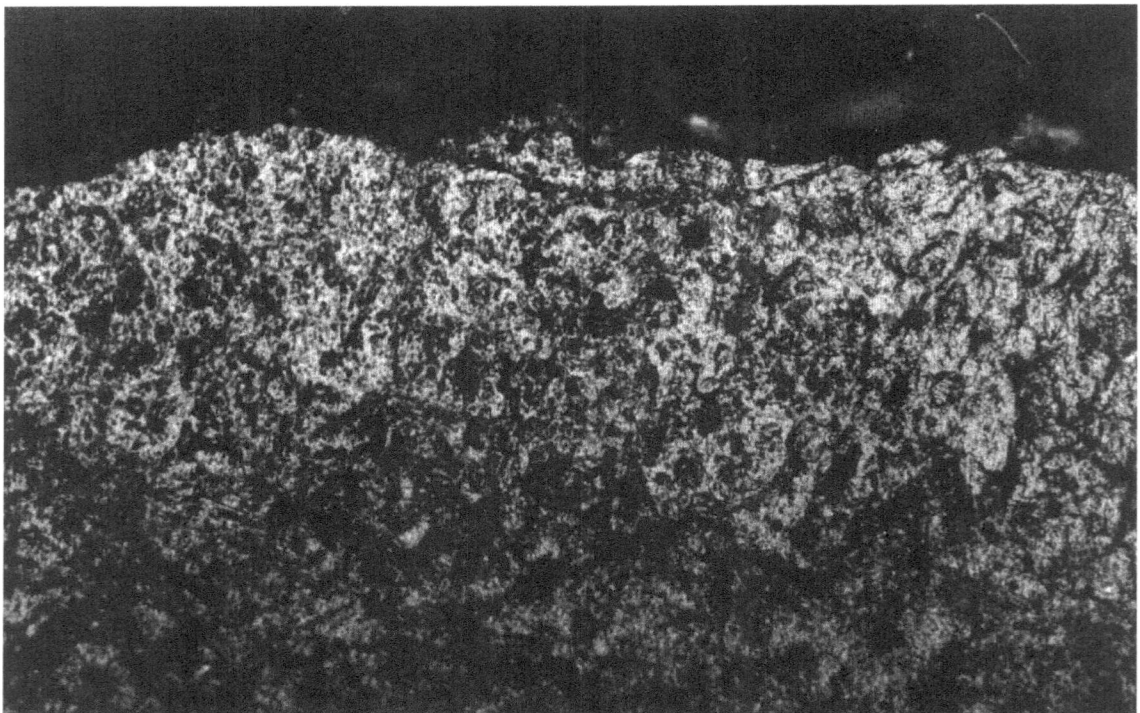

Fig. 5-3 Use-wear polish: hide scraping, ventral side art. #1219-52/82, (200x).

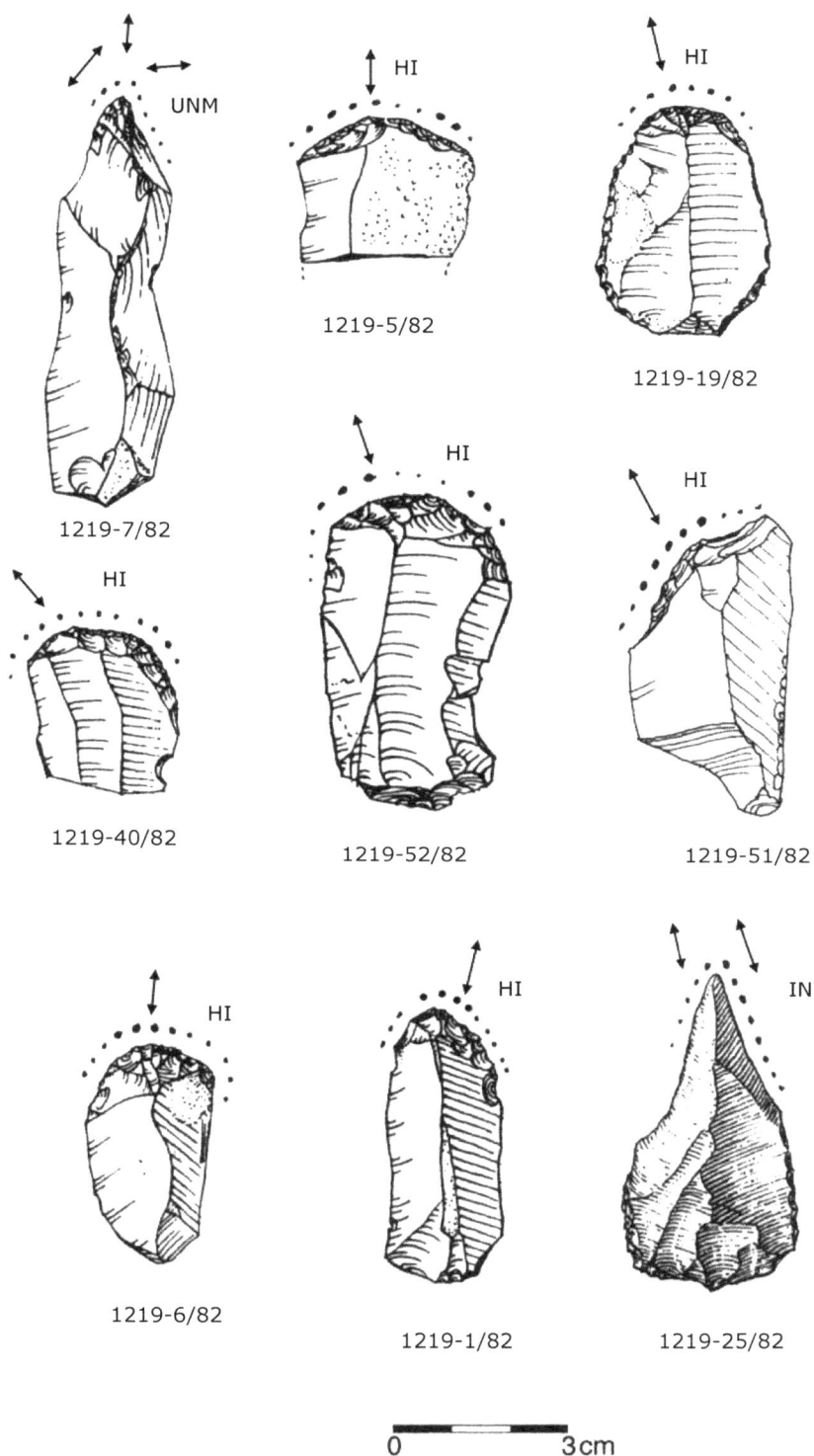

Fig. 5-4 SS III Bohunician artefacts. Drawing by J. Svoboda (2003). The dots indicate the location and intensity of the development of the observed traces. The arrows indicate the direction of the tool motion. Worked materials: HI=hide, UNM= unspecified medium hard, IN=inorganic.

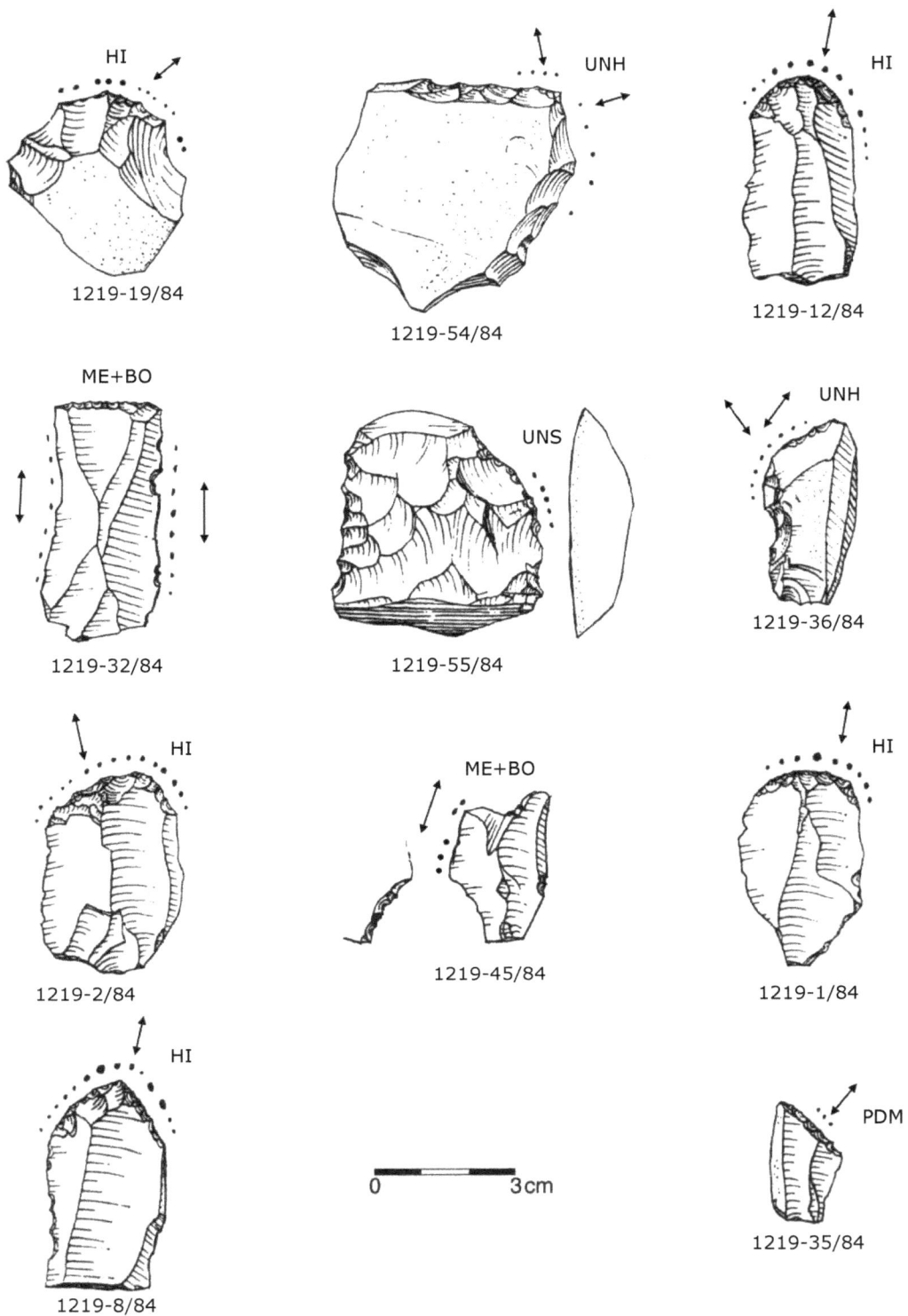

HI
1219-19/84

UNH
1219-54/84

HI
1219-12/84

ME+BO
1219-32/84

UNS
1219-55/84

UNH
1219-36/84

HI
1219-2/84

ME+BO
1219-45/84

HI
1219-1/84

HI
1219-8/84

0 3cm

PDM
1219-35/84

Fig. 5-5 SS IIIa Bohunician artefacts. Drawing by J. Svoboda (2003). The dots indicate the location and intensity of the development of the observed traces. The arrows indicate the direction of the tool motion. Worked materials: HI=hide, UNH= unspecified hard, UNS= unspecified soft, ME+BO=meat+bone, PDM=postdepositional modification.

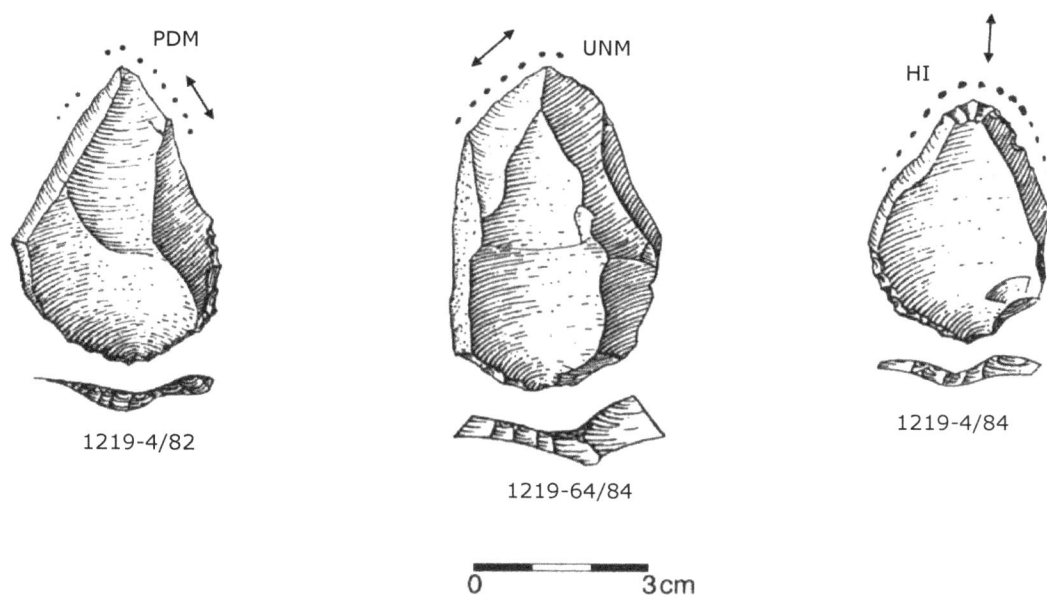

Fig. 5-6 SS III and IIIa Bohunician, Levallois artefacts. Drawing by J. Svoboda (2003). The dots indicate the location and intensity of the development of the observed traces. The arrows indicate the direction of the tool motion. Worked materials: HI=hide, UNM= unspecified medium hard, PDM=postdepositional modification.

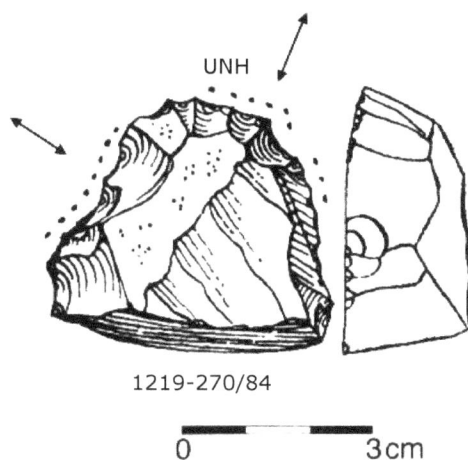

Fig. 5-7 SS IIIa Aurignacian artefact. Drawing by J. Svoboda (2003). The dots indicate the location and intensity of the development of the observed traces. The arrows indicate the direction of the tool motion. Worked material: UNH=unspecified hard.

6. The late Upper Palaeolithic and Mesolithic settlement of the karstic areas

The excavations of the karstic areas in Bohemia and Moravia have taken place over 130 years. However, the scarce and episodic hunters' visits in caves and rock shelters (abri) after the Magdalenian were often overlooked in the archaeological evidence. The new systematic researches since 70s, which have included sieving and soil washing, have revealed not only chipped artefacts but provided other scientific documentation about changes of climate and landscape during the late Upper Palaeolithic and Mesolithic, which is necessary to understand the time period around and after Pleistocene/Holocene boundary (Horáček et al. 2002).

The analysed artefacts came from the soil deposit samples picked by scientists and therefore their evidence probably represents only a fragment of the original,

archeologically inconspicuous, settlements with typical microlithic implements. During the late Upper Palaeolithic and Mesolithic, the karstic areas were supposed to serve as short term, temporary, hunting stations. Archaeological records support the lack of permanent settlements in karstic areas. The microwear analysis attempted to give a glimpse of the functional (apparently hunting) specialisation of the excavated sites interspersed over the Czech Republic (districts Břeclav, Blansko, Prostějov and Beroun).

The final monograph "Prehistorické jeskyně" (Svoboda, ed.) including the results of microwear analysis was published in Dolnověstonické studie 7 (Horáček et al. 2002).

6.1 Material and sampling

The Research Center for Paleolithic and Paleoethnology in Dolní Věstonice, the Institute of Archaeology ASCR in Brno, provided a total of 33 pieces of chipped industry originating from the excavation of the caves: Průchodnice 1989 (7/6), Barová sector 1984 (7/3), Svatý Jan pod skalou - Za křížem 1989 (5/2), Klentnice-Soutěska 1970 (14/13). The first number represents the total amount of artefacts provided, the second one represents the amount of artefacts pre-selected for analysis.

The pre-selection was made by following criteria connected with the probability of the possible usage of the artefact. The criteria were based on those used by other analysts (e.g. Gijn 1990; Juel Jensen and Petersen 1995):

- retouch size < 1 mm (i.e. "use-retouch", mostly connected with the tool use)
- retouch size of 1 mm or bigger (intentional retouch)
- naked eye visible polish
- straight edge (length at least 1 cm)
- protruding point

Based on the above criteria, a total of 24 artefacts (19 flints (79%), 1 radiolarite, 1 quartz, 1 crystal, 2 unknown) were chosen for the microanalysis. The detailed raw material and typological group distribution is presented in Tab. 6-1. The retouched pieces made up about 17% of the analysed implements (12% of the total provided collection).

Tab. 6-1 Distribution of the typological groups and the raw materials.

Typology group	Flint	Radiolarite	Quartz	Crystal	Unknown	Total
Flakes	8				1	9
Blades	4	1		1		6
Microliths	5		1			6
Burins	1					1
Burin spalls	1					1
Cores					1	1
Total count	19	1	1	1	2	24

6.2 Results and discussion

Most of the artefacts display varying but predominantly a high degree of white patina which occasionally exhibited the "sugary" structure described by Schmalz (1960). The second most frequent postdepositional modification was friction gloss (bright spots of different sizes) like in the case of the previously analysed Palaeolithic assemblages (see the previous chapters, for friction gloss origin refer to chapter 2.9). Another difficulty was the presence of graphite on the tool edges and in the microscars. In particular, the artefacts from the site Klentnice had the edges intensively contoured with graphite which highly impaired the analysis. The graphite cannot be fully removed from the surface and remains mainly in the microscars on the edges (Fig. 6-2). Therefore, possible use-wear traces could be hidden by the graphite layer and thus overlooked.

From the preselected sample, 21 pieces of the 24 analysed implements showed no use-wear traces which was about 88%; recalculated for the whole sample it made up over 90%. Interpretable signs of use-wear were traced only on 3 pieces (Tab. 6-2).

Tab. 6-2 Degree of the interpreted use-wear traces plus a composition of the retouched pieces in the analysed samples.

Use-wear traces	
Not interpretable	0% (0%)
Interpretable traces	12,5% (9%)
No traces	87,5% (91%)
Retouched pieces	17% (12%)
% of used retouched pieces	31%

Notes:
 x% - values of analysed samples
(x%) - recalculated values for the primary sample

The excavated sites in the karstic areas were considered as very short term or occasionally settled places and the low percentage of used tools could correspond with that hypothesis. The results are lower than those for Dolní Věstonice II 1999 (see the previous chapter, Tab. 4-3), showing that the karst settlements were probably even more incidental, without specific working activities which would leave used/destroyed tools there. This is most obvious from the development of the use-wear traces, where no extensively or mildly used pieces were found (Tab. 6-4). The typological structure is rather similar to Dolní Věstonice 1999; only "hunter" type tools or flakes left by the manufacture of tools were found.

Tab. 6-3 Degree of development of the interpreted use-wear traces.

Degree of traces	
Unsure/possible use	80%
Light use	20%
Medium use	0%
Extensive use	0%

Some of the examined artefacts could have had more than one used area or could have been retooled – the rest of the originally used areas could still be visible. Two blades displayed 2 actually used areas (AUAs), i.e. both edges were used, but the traces were of unsure character. The third positively interpreted tool (also a blade) had just one recognized AUA.

The distribution of the tool fragments in the analysed samples was very unequal; the complete tools made up nearly 50% of the analysed tools, other fragments had almost the same distribution, between 12%-15%. In contrast to the results of the previous analyses, the traces were observed only on the complete tools (Tab.6-4).

Tab. 6-4 Distribution of the tool fragments and the location of the use-wear traces.

Fragment	% of analysed sample	% of used fragments
Complete	46%	42%
Distal	15%	0%
Medial	12%	0%
Proximal	15%	0%
Unsure	12%	0%

The overview of the interpreted traces categorised by the hardness of the worked material (LPA) is presented in Tab. 6-5. The overview of the interpreted traces using the HPA method is presented in Tab. 6-6. Two positively interpreted artefacts were from the Klentnice cave and one from the Průchodnice cave. No use-wear traces were interpreted on the artefacts from the other sites. The observed traces suggest short usage of the tools as use-wear was only lightly developed. Therefore, the interpretability of the worked material is also limited. All observed use-wear traces were interpreted as the longitudinal direction of working motion.

Tab. 6-5 Interpretation of the use-wear traces using a binocular microscope (LPA).

Typology group	Medium hard	Soft material	Total AUAs	No traces (pieces)
Blades	3	2	5	3
Flakes				9
Burins				1
Microliths				6
Other				2
Total count	3	2	5	21
% of total AUAs	60%	40%		
Total % of analysed pieces	13%	8%		88%

Tab. 6-6 Interpretation of the worked materials using an incident light microscope (HPA).

Typology group	Unspecific soft organic material	Unsure	Total AUAs	No traces (pieces)
Blades	1	4	5	3
Flakes				9
Burins				1
Microliths				6
Other				2
Total count	1	4	5	21
% of total AUAs	20%	80%		
Total % of analysed pieces	4%	17%		88%

6.3 Conclusion

The microwear analysis proved the anticipated short term character of the hunting stations in the karstic areas during the late Upper Palaeolithic and Mesolithic. The low percentage of used artefacts together with the light development of the interpreted traces and the prevalence of unused flakes support the notion that the stations were used as hunting camps where no specialized long term working activities took place. The unused pieces are probably waste products of occasional tool manufacturing.

Unfortunately, the low percentage of used pieces did not allow any contextual interpretation of the use-wear traces but their character (development, longitudinal motion) was in concordance with the expected hunting activities. In any case, the low amount of found pieces in the excavated sites would make any microwear result only illustrative.

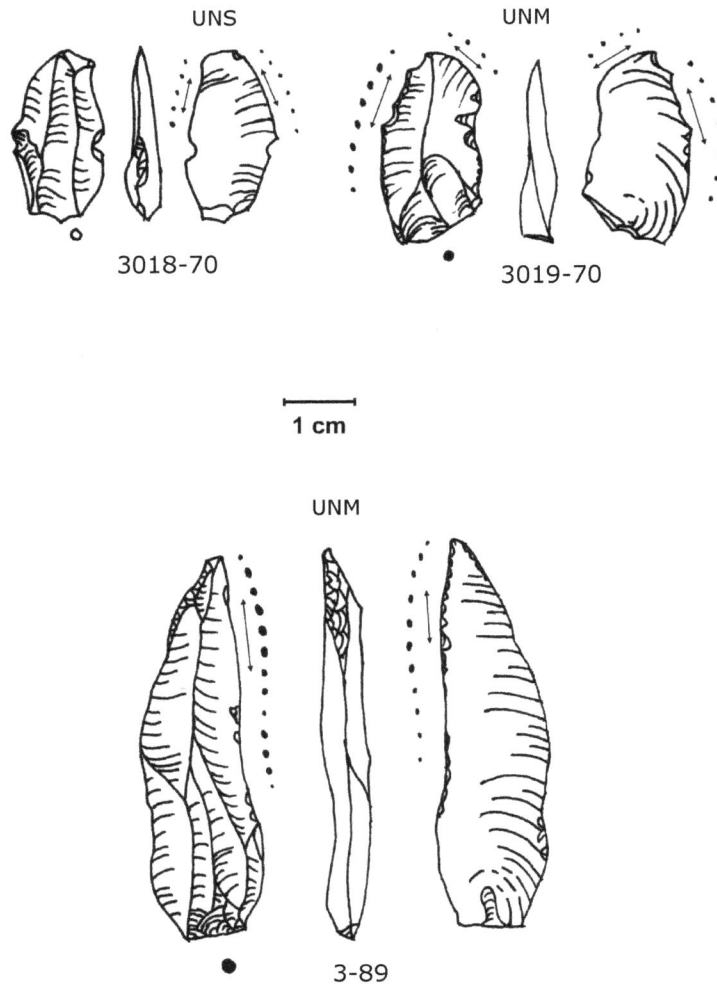

Fig. 6-1 Tools with interpretable use-wear traces. The dots indicate the location and intensity of the development of the observed traces. The arrows indicate the direction of the tool motion. Worked materials: UNS=unspecified soft, UNM=unspecified medium hard.

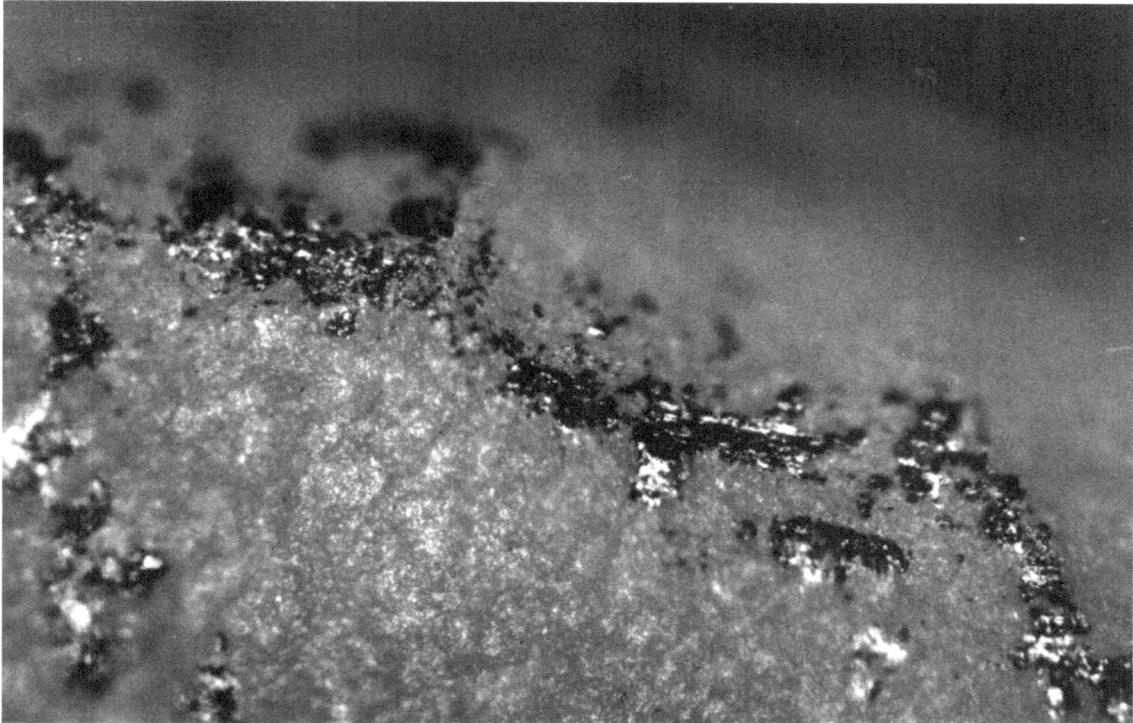

Fig. 6-2 Graphite layer on surface, art.#301-2/70, mag. 100x.

Fig. 6-3 Use-wear polish: cutting medium hard material, art.#3-89, mag. 200x.

Fig. 6-4 Use-wear polish: cutting medium hard material, art.#3-89, mag. 200x.

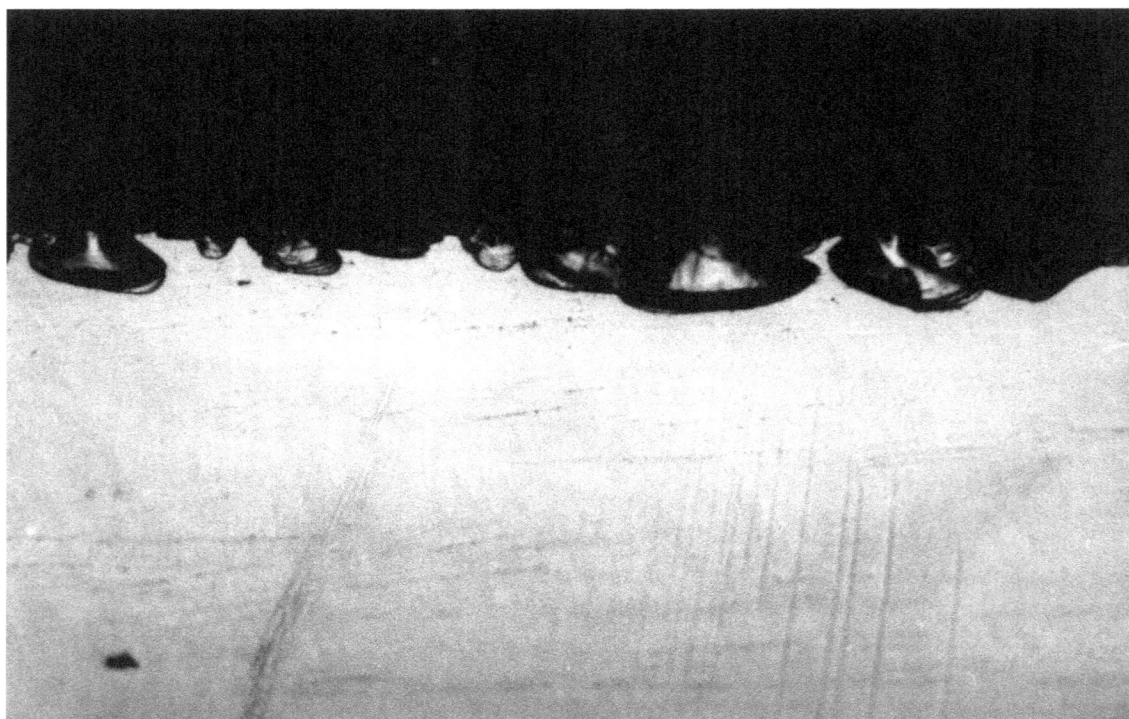

Fig. 6-5 Postdepositional scaring and striation, art.#3-84 (crystal rock), mag. 100x.

7. Discussion: Function, morphology and settlement

The function of tools is often preconceived by the tool typology name, based on the ethnological or archaeological notion. Nevertheless, this should not be taken into consideration during the functional microanalysis as some unexpected locations of the use could be overlooked as the blind test had shown (Unrath et al. 1986). The level of difference of the tool anticipated function and the typological name differ depending on the level of the "punctuality" of the activity description. For example, if a scraper function was interpreted as

whittling, one can suppose it to be in contradiction with the tool typology. However, if we consider both scraping and whittling as two varieties of the transversal motion, the tool function is corresponding with the tool typology or morphology. Such variability can be found with almost all typological groups. Several researches have explored possible correlations between the tool morphology and worked material and, in some instances, positive conclusions have been reached (e.g. Keeley 1978; Juel Jensen 1982; Moss 1983a; Dumont 1986).

7.1 Hafting

Hafting traces are not, with the sole exception of identifiable adhesives, recognised on the artefact surface but rather are deduced according to the observed traces which were not likely to be the result of the use or any other circumstances, such as manufacture or deposition within the site soil. It is not easy to recognize a "standard" pattern or array of traces that could be interpreted as being due to a haft (Keeley 1982). Such traces usually represent the wear on tools that makes a little sense as traces of utilization, but it does conform to what is known as or expected of wear from minor movements of a tool against its haft (Cahen et al. 1979; Keeley 1987). However, experimental programs centred on the formation and possible interpretation of hafting traces have been launched (e.g. Rots 2003, 2004). The presence of potential hafting traces can identify the hafting material (e.g. bone, wood, antler, hide etc.). The distribution of the hafting traces is limited by the extent of contact with the haft across the tool surface, but does not necessary reflect the total extent of the haft.

The absence of potential hafting traces does not indicate the absence of a former haft. It is frequent that the extent of the contact between the haft and the tool, or the morphology of the haft itself, is assumed just by the function of the tool and extension of the regular use-wear traces. But the hafting traces cannot show the shape of the haft beyond its minimum extent across the tool.

The most desirable is to recognise the hafting for microliths to understand their function as the functional traces are insufficient to enable a specific functional interpretation. For these reasons it is instructive to

consider the preserved archaeological examples of hafted microliths, e.g. Mesolithic sites in Scandinavia (Larsson 1983, Clark 1975). The microliths were not exclusively hafted as projectile armatures. Clark (1975) illustrated a uniserially slotted bone knife with inset microblades from Bloksbjerg, Zealand. An extensive discussion of the various types of microliths hafts can be found in Clarke (1976).

Possible positive haft traces were interpreted on a minor part of analysed implements in Pavlov (16 pieces), Dolní Věstonice (3 pieces) and Stránská skála (1 piece). All traces were of the unsure character so the haft material could not be interpreted. The prevalent typological group with the hafting traces was the proximal part of blades (Tab.7-1). Logically, the other tool groups represented the complete pieces or distal fragments, as for example the endscraper, when it was broken, it would be identified only by the "scraper" retouch and the proximal fragment would be interpreted as a broken blade.

Tab. 7-1 Distribution of the hafting traces according to typology and fragments.

Typological group	Fragment	Amount
Blades	complete	2
	proximal	10
	distal	1
Burin	complete	1
	proximal	1
Endscraper	complete	2
	distal	1
Notch	distal	1

7.2 Scrapers

The endscrapers have always played an important role in the study of lithic assemblages because of their abundance and distinctive morphology. Together with projectile points, endscrapers often constitute the backbone of chronological studies. Furthermore, their formal resemblance of certain tools known from current ethnographic has added to the attractiveness of the endscrapers and made them a stand out as intelligible objects in tool assemblages which are otherwise difficult to decode in terms of their use. Thus, prehistoric scrapers are explicitly or implicitly frequently associated with hide working to the point that the semifunctional designation "scraper" has been replaced by the hyperfunctional "hide-working tool" in the caption of the distributional maps (Juel Jensen 1988). Naturally, fascination with endscrapers has been transferred to use-wear analysts and the tool has constituted one of the most intensively analysed lithic implements (e.g. Rosenfed 1971; Bordes 1973; Brink 1978b; Rigaud 1977; Juel Jensen 1982; Gendel 1982).

However, the functions of scrapers need to be assessed through individual microwear analyses rather than by assumptions based on gross morphology or analogy with microwear studies of other site assemblages. The wear studies yield few surprising results concerning the relation between the "scraping edge" and the functionally active area. In most recorded cases, the retouched front had been the active edge used with a scraping or whittling motion, perpendicular to the retouched edge. Nevertheless, in some cases the "scraping edge" appears to have served only as a resting platform for the finger, while the marginal side of the tool was the active edge, used for cutting, whittling or grooving motion (e.g. Juel Jensen 1982; Moss 1983a; Schulte and Strzoda 1985).

The scrapers could have been used for various activities/functions. Although hide, bone, antler and wood were worked by these at most sites, the relative frequency varied considerably. At Star Carr (Mesolithic site) the hide working accounted for 40% of the identifiable use-wear traces, followed by bone and antler-working 22% each and woodworking 13% (Dumont 1987). The used parts were found on the steeply retouched scraping edge and/or the lateral margins of the tools. This indicates that although the preparation of a steeply retouched scraping edge may reflect the maker's intent to use this portion of the tool, its actual use as a working edge cannot be generally assumed on morphological or typological grounds. Dumont (1987) stated that it was possible to make statistically significant general statements concerning one particular aspect of tool morphology, the curvature of the utilised edge in plan view, and the type of material worked by the artefacts: the antler-working edges were less curved

(virtually straight) than those used against hide or bone; the bone-working edges were less curved than those used against hide but more curved than those used against antler; and the hide working edges were more curved than any of the others.

Similar results were obtained by Moss (1983a) when she examined endscrapers from Pincevent (Late Magdalenian site) and from Pont D'Ambon (Late Magdalenian and Azilian rock shelter). The analysed endscrapers were primarily used for scraping of hide (87%) while the remaining parts were used against other materials. The steeply retouched edges were utilised for hide working, the lateral margins for hide scraping and cutting, wood planing and butchering. With regard to the tool morphology and function, Moss (1983a) demonstrated that the hide-working scrapers were significantly shorter that those used against other materials.

Juel Jensen (1982) analysed endscrapers from the Danish late Mesolithic site of Ringkloster (Ertebølle) and received interesting results. 93% of the analysed pieces exhibited the use of the steeply retouched edge for scarping. The remainder, lacking the utilisation of the formal "scraper edge", exhibited the use of the lateral margins for wood and meat-working. However, 60% of the endscrapers used on the "scraper edge" shoved additional use of the lateral margins primarily against wood but also plant. Morphologically, the scrapers could be divided into two groups (complete and broken) that correlate with a clear functional difference. 81% of the complete scrapers were used for hide-working, while 72% of the broken scrapers were used for woodworking. Furthermore, the woodworking scrapers were slightly thinner than the hide-working tools. Jensen (1982) suggests that the broken tools were intentionally manufactured to this final form for use against wood. Similarly, at other Mesolithic site Vænget Nord 70% of the analysed scrapers were used for hide-working, 10% for woodworking and 10% for working of the unidentified hard material (Juel Jensen and Petersen 1985).

Very similar results for the interpreted worked materials frequency, the topography of the used areas and morphological differences (denticulated/irregular edge for woodworking vs. regular one for hide-working) were reported by Keeley (1981), Plisson (1982) and Gendel (1982). However, it is necessary to keep in mind that sometimes it is not clear whether the additional functions (except using the scraper edge) were performed before the creation of the scraper edge, during the functional life of the scraper edge or after the tool ceased being a "scraper" from the tool user's perspective.

The proportional frequency of working hide, relative to the other interpreted contact materials reported in functional studies, indicates an abrupt change in the use patterns when comparing Upper/Late Palaeolithic and Mesolithic/Neolithic materials. The multifunctional role of a scraper as a type seems to begin only at the onset of the Mesolithic, while the Upper and Late Palaeolithic endscrapers appear to be used almost exclusively as hide-working implements (Juel Jensen 1988). This corresponds with the fact that wood-working traces, frequently found on Mesolithic and Neolithic endscrapers, are almost nonexistent in the Upper and Final Palaeolithic assemblages. In spite of the glacial period, this information is somewhat surprising. Moss (1983a) points out that the lack of evidence is partially accounted for the sampling procedures, since excavations and thus use-wear analyses have been concentrated mainly around "domestic areas". She suggests that wood-working in the Late Palaeolithic was basically confined to heavy-duty work such as making tent poles, drying frames and working firewood, i.e. tasks which require large spaces away from the hearth. If wood had been more plentiful, it might have been employed for the

manufacture of many more objects and some of this manufacture and disposal of tools would have taken place around hearths (as bone and antler working tools did). That radically changed from Mesolithic when the wood as a raw material was used not only in the heavy-duty sphere but also for minor crafts or "domestic activities" as reflected in the use-wear evidence where wood becomes a commonly encountered contact material on flint tool edges including scraper-fronts (Gendel 1982; Juel Jensen 1982; Dumond 1983). It seems that the use pattern displayed by endscrapers is closely connected with the specific economic and ecological setting of the individual site.

The above results closely correspond with the results obtained in this research on 88 analysed scrapers. Hide was the most often worked material as in other Palaeolithic studies (Tab. 7-2). Only 4% of the analysed scrapers did not display any use-wear traces. Also, the functional difference between sidescrapers and endscrapers was more than obvious.

Tab. 7-2 The distribution of worked material by scrapers.

Worked material	Total	Endscraper	Endscraper + burin	Sidescraper
Hide	76%	80%	89%	30%
Unspecific soft	9%	9%		20%
Bone/wood	1%	1%		
Soft wood	1%	1%		
Unspecific hard	6%	3%	11%	20%
Unspec. medium hard	2%	1%		10%
Unsure	1%	1%		
No traces	4%	3%		20%

The proportion of distal fragments and of complete tools of scrapers was almost equivalent. However, it is interesting that the not used pieces were more often in the category of the complete tools. In addition, the other materials except hide made up the same proportion of traces for both complete tools and the distal fragments (Tab. 7-3).

Tab. 7-3 The distribution of the fragments and the interpreted traces.

Scraper fragment	Total (pieces)	Used	Hide	Other
Complete	40	93%	75%	18%
Distal	45	98%	80%	18%
Unsure	3	100%	100%	0%

The edge angles did not reveal any significant morphological correlation between the used materials in analysed samples but that is probably due to a low amount of other worked materials except hide (Tab. 7-4).

The functional area of the analysed scrapers was predominantly the retouched "scraping" edge. The longitudinal motions were found exclusively on the lateral edges and made up only about 4% of the interpreted motions (Tab. 7-5). To compare it with another Gravettian site Willendorf II, it is interesting that Tomášková (2000) did not observe any longitudinal use-wear traces either on endscrapers or sidescrapers in her analysed samples.

Tab. 7-4 The used edge angles according to the interpreted traces and motions.

Worked material	Longitudinal motion			Transversal motion			Unsure direction		
	Min	Max	Avg.	Min	Max	Avg.	Min	Max	Avg.
Hide	45°	45°	45°	24°	104°	68°			
Unspecific soft				59°	87	71°	47°	47°	47°
Bone/wood				54°	54°	54°			
Soft wood				77°	77°	77°			
Unspecific hard	24°	64°	44°	54°	76°	67°	62°	62°	62°
Unspec medium hard	31°	31°	31°				64°	64°	64°
Unsure				65°	77°	71°			

Tab. 7-5 The location of the used area according to the interpreted motions.

Used area	Longitudinal motion	Transversal motion	Unsure direction	Total
Lateral edges	4%	1%	1%	6%
Scraping edge		92%	2%	94%
Total	4%	93%	3%	100%

7.3 Burins

Burins constitute a heterogeneous class of implements whose common denominator is the burin blow technique. Further typological subdivisions are based on the position of the burin bevel and on the method of preparing the striking platform for the burin blow. The anticipation for burins usage is usually bone/antler-working, with incising as the most frequent activity based on theories focused on the burin bit and its capability of engraving and grooving hard materials (e.g. Clark and Thompson 1958; Movius 1968). This activity has been demonstrated in almost all assemblages where burins have been analysed.

Nevertheless, some studies determined that other actions were employed as well. It is also apparent that the burin facet margins and the lateral sides of the burins could have been considered by the tool users potentially functional edges, mainly employed for planning and/or shaving of hard substances. These findings correspond with the theories which stress the functional meaning of the burin facet (e.g. Bordes 1965; Rigaud 1972; Newcomer 1974). In general, both of these modes of use were anticipated or could be inferred from the negative imprints made by the tool edges on bone or antler artefacts. Less expected are the piercing and boring activities displayed by burin bits in several Palaeolithic assemblages (Keeley 1978; Moss 1983a; Juel Jensen and Petersen 1985; Vaughan 1985a, 1985b).

The others have interpreted the burin facet as a blunting or hafting device (e.g. Semenov 1957; Mortensen 1970; Tomášková 2005). The functional interpretations have not yet answered the question if the burin is more a tool or a technique (Juel Jensen 1988).

Dumont (1987) reported burins with use-wear traces only at Starr Carr (Mesolithic), where this tool type was numerous. The burins were used principally against antler but also against bone and unidentified materials. The use activities consisted primarily of incising/planing, sawing and unresolved manners of use. Topographically, about 50% of interpreted use traces were found on the bit while the rest used the long lateral margins of the burins facets. No clear correlations between tool morphology and function emerged from the data. At Pincevent (Magdalenian), Moos (1983) determined that the burins bits and facet margins were used for bone/antler-working and hide working. The bone/antler-working tasks consisted of incising, boring and planing while hide-working involved scraping, piercing and cutting. In Mesolithic site Vænget Nord, 67% of the analysed burins exhibited use-wear traces on one or several parts of the tool and except for one case of hide polish, all traces were interpreted as working bone/antler or unspecified hard material; the polish was often weakly developed. The use-wear traces were not limited to burin bit/bevel as 77% of the analysed burins were used to work with the sides of burin facets for bone/antler scraping/shaving (Juel Jensen and Petersen 1985). Those studies have clearly demonstrated that burins were not used solely as the lithic component of the groove and splinter technique of antler/bone-working.

However, a large number of analysed burins showed no traces of use on the burinated section of the tool (Vaughan 1985b; Tomášková 2005). At Magdalenian sites of Cassegros, Ardenach 2 and Zingeunerfels, Vaughan (1985b) reported that many burins (18%–54%)

bore no traces at all. Among the remainder between 30%-55% displayed use-wear anywhere but on the burin edge. In the latter case, the removal of a burin spall often appears to be secondary in relation to the original use of the piece, as the result of resharpening or blunting attempts. There can be several interpretations of the non used burin phenomenon: unsuccessful production attempts, accidental burination, primary production of burin spall with burin being the core, or the specific function which leaves no traces detectable by the methods currently employed (Juel Jensen 1988).

In this study, burins made up almost the same proportion of tools as scrapers. The burin as secondary modification of tools seems to appear at least on the combi tools where no use-wear traces on the "burinated" part were found at all: 9x combination burin-endscraper, 2x combination burin-notch and 1x combination burin-point. The combi burins comprised about 15% of all analysed burins. In accordance with Vaughan report, over 60% of burins did not bear any interpretable use-wear traces (Tab. 7-6, compare with the results of scrapers, Tab. 7-2).

Tab. 7-6 The distribution of worked material by burins.

Worked material	Total	Burin	Combi – burin part
Hide	9%	10%	
Soft animal	1%	2%	
Antler/Ivory	5%	6%	
Soft wood	1%	2%	
Unspecific hard	6%	7%	
Unspec medium hard	4%	4%	
Unsure	8%	9%	
No traces	66%	60%	100%

The proportion of the distal fragments and the complete tools with a burin blow (excluding the combi tools) was almost equal; less frequent were the medial and proximal parts of tools. It is interesting that complete and distal fragments displayed use-wear traces more or less in the same amount, about 50% (Tab. 7-7). The medial fragments seemed to be the least used parts. Although the hard/medium hard materials in general made up the most frequently worked materials, in total 16% of tools (Tab. 7-6), the hard materials seem to be worked more preferably by the complete tools and/or proximal fragments.

The functional area of the analysed burins (excluding the combi tools) was almost equally the lateral edge and the burin bit, the burin bevel was used about half as often.

The graving (diagonal motion) made up only 25% of the interpreted motions (Tab. 7-8). That confirms the multifunctional character of the burin not only as a "graving tool" also in these studies. However, the burin bit is clearly connected with working hard materials and the lateral edges were preferably used for working soft materials and/or hide (Tab. 7-9). In comparison with another Gravettian site Willendorf II, Tomášková (2000) reported the transversal motion as the most frequent working activity of the analysed burins.

In addition, 7 pieces of burin spalls were analysed. One piece displayed the traces of hide scraping and seemed to be a result of rejuvenation or reutilization of a scraping edge. The other pieces did not expose any use-wear traces or traces not interpretable by any of the methods.

Tab. 7-7 The distribution of the fragments and the interpreted traces (combi tools not included).

Burin fragment	Total (pieces)	Used	Hard/medium hard materials	Other
Complete	23	52%	30%	22%
Distal	17	47%	18%	29%
Medial	9	11%	0%	11%
Proximal	10	30%	20%	10%
Unsure	7	29%	0%	29%

Tab. 7-8 The location of the used area according to the interpreted motions.

Used area	Longitudinal motion	Transversal motion	Diagonal motion	Boring/ piercing	Unsure direction	Total
Lateral edge	31%				10%	41%
Burin bit		3%	22%	3%	9%	37%
Burin bevel	3%	13%	3%		3%	22%
Total	34%	16%	25%	3%	22%	100%

Tab. 7-9 The location of the used area according to the interpreted worked material.

Used area	Hard/medium hard material	Soft material/ hide	Unsure	Total
Lateral edge	6%	22%	13%	41%
Burin bit	28%	0%	9%	37%
Burin bevel	10%	6%	6%	22%
Total	44%	28%	18%	100%

7.4 Blades and flakes

Blades together with flakes seem to be the most universal tools, although they are literally not a "real" tool type, according to some typological systems. However, their importance among other tool types was proved just by traceology. These informal tools were used against a range of materials in a variety of ways, depending on the respective site ecological and economical status. Retouched tools reflect only a small fraction of the activities going on at a site. Although, retouched edges can be an effective devise for scraping, graving or chopping of harder or tougher materials a natural, sharp flint edge is the most logical choice for a number of other purposes. Ethno-archaeological investigations of modern lithic industries have yielded numerous examples of the importance of unretouched pieces and similar information has emerged from archaeological records.

Juel Jensen (1984) in her microwear study of blades from Ageröd V (Mesolithic) reported interesting results. 70% of analysed blades were used against vegetal materials and 28% for hide-working in different states (fresh, dry). Juel Jensen was able to make several statements regarding the tool function and morphology. The edge angles of plant working tools ranged between 40° and 50° while the woodworking edge angles had a lower range, between 30° and 45°. Further, she ascertained that the tools users preferred to utilize blades having edge angles between 20° and 55°, and especially within the range of 30° to 45° (Juel Jensen and Petersen 1985). These angles corresponded with the preferred range of the cutting edges reported for unretouched flake tools from modern New Guinea and Australia (Gould et al. 1971, White et al. 1977), thereby supporting the assumption that the edge angles were selected simply according to the utilitarian

needs, i.e. they offered a sharp but at the same time a sufficiently strong edge that would withstand the stresses of the use. The edge angle probably was not the criterion recognized by the tool users but it reflects more general features as thickness or the ratio thickness/widths (Juel Jensen and Petersen 1985).

Dumont (1987) analysed only small samples of the apparently used blades from Star Carr and Mount Sandel (both Mesolithic). At both sites, they were used against a variety of materials (antler, bone, hide, minerals, wood, unidentified materials) in a variety of ways (cutting/sawing, planing, whittling, scraping and unidentified uses). The relative frequencies of the different tasks also varied: whereas the majority (60%) of the Star Carr use-traces consisted of whittling and 20% of scraping/planing, the most frequent task (45% of the interpreted traces) at Mount Sandel consisted of cutting/sawing and 35% of scraping/planing. At both Mont Sandel and Star Carr there was convincing evidence that the tools users selected the more robust blades for use. The utilised artefacts exhibited significantly greater maximum thicknesses and less acute edge angles than the non-utilised artefacts. However, it was not clear whether the less robust blades were used against less demanding materials, such as meat, where traces may not be sufficiently well developed for recognition. The mean edge angle was 50° for Star Carr blades and 45° for those from Mount Sandel.

Tomášková (2000) in her analysis of the blades from Willendorf II (Gravettian) reported a different percentage of the used blades in 5 cultural layers (layer 5 to layer 9). The portion varied from 25% in layer 5 and 6 to 42-3% of used blades in layer 7 and 8 and 32% in layer 9. The worked materials were mostly the fresh organic materials. Tomášková explained the differences in the percentage of the used blades by different short term seasonal settlements in every layer.

In this study, blades were the most plentiful tool category in the analysed samples and made up about 42% of all analysed implements, unlike flakes which formed only about 10% of the analysed pieces. About 50% of them wore traces of use (Tab. 7-9). A special type, the backed blades, follows more the concept of the tool in the view of typology. The function of those tools usually does not differ from normal blades, although their usage seems to be more specialized and varies at every excavated site (e.g. Dumont 1987, Cahen et al. 1979). In this study the retouched blades (backed, crested or with a local retouch) constituted only 12% of all analysed blades and their usage seemed to be more specialized to working soft (animal) materials and hide. Therefore, they were combined into one category "retouched blades" for further comparisons including the truncated blades (see below). The percentage composition of tools used for working hide and soft animal materials was identical to unretouched blades, but the latter were used also for working hard materials (Tab. 7-9).

The typological group of retouched truncated blades used to be considered functionally different and much closer to scrapers. Therefore, their utilisation should correspond more with the results obtained for scrapers (cf. Dumont 1987). Similar results were obtained at the Mesolithic site of Vænget Nord where 41% of analysed truncated blades were used for hide-working (cutting and scraping), 8% for working siliceous plants and 8% for mixture of hide and plant working (Juel Jensen and Petersen 1985). In this study only two truncated blades from the Stránská skála excavation were analysed and one of which was interpreted as used for butchering, the other did not display any interpretable use-wear traces. Therefore, this presumption about the functional similarity of the truncated blades and scrapers could not be confirmed for

Palaeolithic assembles from the analysed sites in the Czech Republic, but only 2 pieces are obviously too few to draw any final conclusions.

Tab. 7-9 The distribution of worked material by blades.

Worked material	Total	Blank blades	Retouched blades
Hide	17%	17%	17%
Unspecific/animal soft	13%	13%	13%
Antler/Ivory	1%	1%	
Wood	1%	2%	
Unspecific hard	3%	3%	
Unspec. medium hard	8%	9%	7%
Inorganic soft	1%	1%	
Unsure	7%	8%	7%
No traces	49%	48%	57%

The complete blades were the most frequent category followed by the proximal fragments. However, the proximal fragments categorized as blades might be complementary pieces of other tool types like endscrapers or others. The distal blade fragments made up about half of the analysed complete blades. However, it is interesting that the used wear traces seem to be more likely to be found on the broken fragments of blades, especially, on the distal or medial parts (Tab. 7-10). The not used pieces were more often present in the category of the complete tools. In addition, the hide or unspecific soft/animal materials made up to about half of the interpreted traces on all fragments except for a very slight difference for the complete tools (Tab. 7-10).

The edge angles did not reveal any significant morphological correlations between the contact materials worked in the same direction of motion but they showed that there was a considerable difference in the angle of the used edge between the transversal and longitudinal motions (Tab. 7-11).

Tab. 7-10 The distribution of the blade fragments and the interpreted traces.

Blade fragment	Total (pieces)	Used	Hide or soft/animal materials	Other
Complete	89	43%	25%	18%
Distal	42	64%	33%	31%
Medial	23	65%	30%	35%
Proximal	74	49%	27%	22%
Unsure	2	50%	50%	0%

Tab. 7-11 The used blade edge angles according to the interpreted traces and motions.

Worked material	Longitudinal motion			Transversal motion			Unsure direction/ hafting		
	Min	Max	Avg.	Min	Max	Avg.	Min	Max	Avg.
Hide	16°	54°	38°	31°	79°	58°			
Soft	16°	61°	37°						
Medium hard	29°	44°	39°				47°	54°	51°
Hard	25°	30°	28°	37°	52°	44°	33°	41°	39°
Unsure	22°	56°	39°				33°	48°	38°

Flakes comprised only about 10% of analysed artefacts but this amount is comparable with the other bigger typological groups like scrapers and burins. About 8% of the analysed flakes were retouched. The range of worked materials was similar to those worked by blades (Tab. 7-12) but a smaller percentage of flake tools were used in general.

Complete implements dominated the analysed sample of flakes (Tab. 7-13). However, the use-wear traces were more often found on the distal fragments. The distribution of worked materials by the different fragments did not reveal any significant differences. It is interesting that harder materials comprised lesser portion of use-wear traces interpreted on flakes than on blades (cf. Tab. 7-10).

The angles of the used edges of flakes, similarly to blades, indicate the difference between the transversal

and longitudinal motion (Tab. 7-14). However, due to low amount of the used flakes these results are only illustrative.

Tab. 7-12 The distribution of worked material by flakes.

Worked material	Total	Blank flakes	Retouched flakes
Hide	15%	14%	25%
Unspecific soft	6%	4%	25%
Antler/Ivory	2%	2%	0%
Wood	2%	2%	0%
Unspecific hard	2%	2%	0%
Unspec medium hard	2%	2%	0%
Unsure	4%	0%	50%
No traces	69%	74%	0%

Tab. 7-13 The distribution of the fragments and the interpreted traces.

Flake fragment	Total (pieces)	Used	Hide or soft/animal materials	Other
Complete	32	34%	22%	13%
Distal	7	57%	43%	14%
Proximal	4	0%		
Unsure	11	27%	18%	9%

Tab. 7-14 The used edge angles according to the interpreted traces and motions.

Worked material	Longitudinal motion			Transversal motion			Unsure direction		
	Min	Max	Avg.	Min	Max	Avg.	Min	Max	Avg.
Hide				44°	93°	64°	50°	50°	50°
Soft	27°	42°	32°	65°	65°	65°			
Medium hard							31°	31°	31°
Hard	24°	24°	24°						
Unsure				54°	54°	54°	71°	71°	71°

7.5 Points

Absence of wear traces on points does not necessarily indicate that they were not used. Available experimental evidence demonstrate that only a proportion of fired points/arrow tips will yield diagnosable impact traces, depending on whether or not the projectile hit a hard substance as bone or sinew. The results indicate that a possible previous use of projectile points can be ascertained for about 66% of the used pieces (Moss and Newcomer 1982; Moss 1983a; Fisher et al. 1984; Gijn 1990).

In Mesolithic site Vænget Nord 43% of the analysed points exhibited linear impact traces parallel to the longitudinal axis. None of these pieces showed use polishes on one or several portions of the tool, except for one case of hide polish. All traces were interpreted as working bone/antler or unspecified hard material, but the polish was often weakly developed (Juel Jensen and Petersen 1985).

In this study points represented rather a minor group of analysed implements, only about 3% (18 pieces). Therefore, the presented results can be considered only as for orientation. Use-wear traces were ascertained on low portion of points, from 56% to 22% of analysed pieces depending on the point type and the selected sample (Tab. 7-15). Most of traces were of unsure character, only

two use-wear traces were developed into a medium degree.

Tab. 7-15 The distribution of worked material by points.

Worked material	Total	Levallois points	Other points
Hide	11%	0%	22%
Unspecific soft	6%	0%	11%
Unspec. medium hard	11%	22%	0%
Unsure	11%	0%	22%
No traces	61%	78%	44%

The complete points were the most frequent category followed by the distal fragments, probably because the proximal fragments could have been categorised as a different tool type, similarly to e.g. endscrapers. Logically, the distal fragments were more often interpreted as used as the point tip or the distal part should be the expected functional area of points (Tab. 7-16).

Although the tip of the point is considered the main functional area, the traces were more often found on the lateral edges (Tab. 7-17). However, the difference cannot be considered significant due to the low amount of the analysed points.

Tab. 7-16 The distribution of the fragments and the interpreted traces.

Point fragment	Total (pieces)	Used	Hide or soft/animal materials	Other
Complete	10	30%	0%	30%
Distal	6	50%	50%	0%
Medial	1	100%	0%	100%
Proximal	1	0%		

Tab. 7-17 The location of the used area according to the interpreted motions.

Used area	Longitudinal motion	Dynamic activities	Unsure direction	Total
Lateral edges	40%	0%	20%	60%
Tip	10%	20%	10%	40%
Total	50%	20%	30%	100%

7.6 Microliths

By microliths are meant any small, 2-3 cm long (but often even shorter), stone artefacts deliberately retouched, made generally from bladelet blanks. Microliths were a typical and frequent tool type in the Gravettian lithic industry. Unfortunately, we are still not able to fully understand their function due to the dearth of the functional information available from the microwear analysis, not only in this research but also according to other researches and reports about different sites from different periods of time when the microliths were a part of the lithic assemblages. Microliths manufacture appears to follow a very general design pattern; variations in tool form appear to be relatively insignificant. The selection of microliths for the use appears to relate to the desired morphological traits and not to the intended end use (Finlayson and Mithen 1997). This may reinforce the notions that the microlith represents a standardized plug-in, replaceable component in composite tools, whether they are projectiles or some of the non-hunting alternatives suggested by Clarke (1976). In Mesolithic, a period of archery hunting, the microliths had been widely assumed to be used as the tips and barbs of arrows. Although, the archery is not too often considered in the Gravettian, the microliths usage as presumed weapon tips was still considered (e.g. Straus 2002).

Dumont (1987) reported less than 7% (2/31) of analysed pieces from Star Carr (Mesolithic) that exhibited possible use-wear traces - potential hafting traces. The analysed microliths from the rich excavation made at Mount Sandel (Mesolithic) brought slightly interesting results. About 16% (25/157) of the exhibited traces were attributed either to the use or to the former presence of a haft. Dumond (1987) determined that except for the three backed bladelets the functional traces (including impact fractures) were consistent with a presumed use of microliths as weapon armatures. The three exceptions were used for stone, hide and woodworking. Similar conclusions were reached by Moss (1983a) concerning the Pincevent (Magdalenian) backed bladelets. In her opinion, the primary function of these tools was being used as projectile barbs and points. Several backed bladelets though were apparently used to cut and pierce hide. Keeley (1981, 1987) interpreted the backed bladelets from Verberie as projectile armatures as well.

On the contrary, Finlayson and Mithen (1997) in the research from the Mesolithic site of Gleann Mor (Scotland) reported that 38% (46/120) of microliths displayed a sign of use, but only a minority (about 10%) displayed features that are typical for projectile use. The main identified tool motion was longitudinal, a cutting motion (33%), 13% of the microliths had traces associated with a transverse or shaving motion and 13% showed signs of having been used with a rotary motion, as for boring. The traces were significantly associated with scalene triangles with 3 retouched edges and with sharp angles. It is possible that the projectile use could be under-represented, due to pieces lost off site and to pieces not showing wear traces. However, even if these factors were taken into account, the large number of pieces with positive evidence of non-projectile use proved that microliths were not a single function tool form and that they do not equate entirely with the act of hunting. It could be even suggested that the projectile use may be a relatively minor function at this site. No significant functional difference was found between microliths types (Finlayson and Mithen 1997).

The anticipations about the usage of the microliths for dynamic shooting activities is obvious from the prevalent researchers' opinion based mostly on indirect use traces as impact fractures, hafting and polish streaks. However, this could not be applied to this research. The analysed microliths comprised about 10% of the analysed tools, i.e. about the same portion as burins or flakes (Tab. 2-1). The absence of interpretable traces on microliths was very high, as already mentioned in the presented studies of the respective researches. It is interesting that the unretouched pieces were more often interpreted as used than the retouched ones (Tab. 7-18). This can be explained in two ways: either the retouch shaded the weakly developed use-wear traces from the soft materials or the retouched pieces represent the prepared unused replaceable components for composite tools. The unretouched microliths seem to be more often interpreted as used for working the soft animal materials. However, the unretouched pieces comprised only 28% of all analysed microliths.

Tab. 7-18 The distribution of worked material by points.

Worked material	Total	Unretouched microliths	Retouched microliths
Hide	5%	6%	5%
Animal soft tissue	5%	13%	2%
Inorganic/soil	2%	6%	0%
Unsure	5%	6%	5%
No traces	82%	69%	88%

The complete microliths were the most frequent category. All other analysed fragments (medial, distal and proximal) had equal representation (Tab. 7-19). The low presence of interpreted use-wear traces and representation of the fragments (e.g. proximal) makes the percentage results only illustrative.

Tab. 7-19 The distribution of the fragments and the interpreted traces.

Point fragment	Total (pieces)	Used	Hide or soft/animal materials	Other
Complete	32	28%	9%	19%
Distal	8	0%	0%	0%
Medial	8	0%	0%	0%
Proximal	8	13%	13%	0%
Unsure	1	0%	0%	0%

Although the majority of notions consider the microliths to be used as the projectiles, in this study neither traces of dynamic activities nor the impact fractures were found. The use-wear traces were more often found on the lateral edges of the analysed microliths than on the tips (Tab. 7-20). However, the differences cannot be considered significant due to a low presence of interpretable use-wear traces. Although, they could have been used for composed tools, use-wear analysis did not sustain this hypothesis as no hafting traces were found either. If the

microliths were used as tips for harpoons or arrows then the situation with the missing use-wear traces would be similar to the one of the points; the used pieces were probably destroyed or lost outside of the camp.

Similar results, i.e. the prevalence of the longitudinal motion in the use-wear traces on the microliths, were also ascertained in the Willendorf II collection (Tomášková 2000).

Tab. 7-20 The location of the used area according to the interpreted motions.

Used area	Longitudinal motion	Boring/ piercing	Transversal motion	Unsure direction	Total
Lateral edges	43%	0%	0%	29%	72%
Tip	0%	7%	7%	14%	28%
Total	43%	7%	7%	43%	100%

7.7 Settlement type and a degree of development of use-wear traces

One of the questions raised by the excavation of settlements is whether the site was occupied year-round or served as a special purpose camp visited only briefly to exploit one particular resource. There are several ways how use-wear analysis can contribute to the discussion about the duration of the occupancy. Excavations presented in this study showed clear differences in functional interpretation based on analysed assemblages. However, the correlation between the time aspect of the settlement with the observed traces and their development was further analysed to find a feature which would correspond the most. Although the number/percentage of used tools would seem to be a major correlation, there could be a problem with recalculating the samples to the same level, due to the different sampling methods. For example, as the Pavlov excavation was already re-sampled by the excavators with the unknown ration of "wasted" pieces the total percentage of the used pieces can be estimated only approximately. A simple recalculation of the inventoried pieces to the estimated

total amount of all stone pieces would be misleading. In some other studies, which were focused only on several types of tools, this would be even harder.

Solely for demonstration purposes, I attempted to recalculate the results for all of the above analysed sites using the recounted total number of excavated stone pieces (including the estimated bulk material, see chapter 3.1). Surprisingly, the total number of used pieces was more or less constant, about 10-14% (Tab. 7-21) and corresponded with the recalculated results from other sites where a "complete" selection of excavated artefacts for microanalysis was made, e.g. Beek-Molensteeg, the LBK site (10%, N= 1704; Gijn 1990), Vænget Nord, the Mesolithic site (16%, N=846; Jensen and Peterson 1985) or Cassegros, the Magdalenian site (18%, N=855; Vaughan 1985a). Tomášková (2000) reported higher percentage of used tools in excavations of the Gravettian site Willendorf II (from 22% to 38%, depending on the cultural layer, N=2631), however, it is not clear if all excavated pieces were catalogued. It would make sense that the tool manufacture produced more or less constant volume of the chipping debitage which is displayed by unused pieces.

Tab. 7-21 The recalculated estimated percentage of used tools in analysed excavated site where any positive use-wear traces were found.

Excavation	Used pieces
Pavlov 1954A	13%[1]
Pavlov 1957	12%[1]
Pavlov 1970	13%[1]
Pavlov 1971	11%[1]
DV IIa 1999	12%
Průchodnice	14%
Klentnice	14%

[1] The approximate percentage of used pieces in non inventoried debitage in Pavlov was estimated on 10% according to other studies (Moss 1983a; Vaughan 1985a; Symens 1986; Juel Jensen 1986, 1988; Gijn 1990)

As microwear analysis, due to its nature, is not suitable for the primary sorting and investigation of assemblages, the method is almost always forced to operate with small samples of the available archaeological material. The entire assemblage is examined only exceptionally, when the total number of excavated pieces does not exceed the reasonable amount (e.g. Vaughan 1985a). It seems that the small differences in the percentage of used pieces would rather depend on the type of sampling and on the completeness of the excavation in general. Therefore, other features were tested to compare their presence in different types of settlements. Using the relative ratio would allow to compare the results and make them independent on the proportion of the used tools.

Distribution of a degree of the development of use-wear traces in the analysed assemblage is basically dependent on the type of sampling; however, the results are more independent of the total percentage of used/unused pieces characteristics. Thus, the excavation with a similar sampling could be more easily compared using this characteristic. Of course, the problem is that the category is relative, subjectively stated by every analyst. However, the results in comparison with the other researches can be interesting. For comparison, the results determined by Gijn (1990) for the permanent settlement in Beek-Molensteeg (LBK) and recurrent seasonal settlement in Hekelingen III (Late Neolithic) are shown in Tab. 7-22. Interestingly, the results of the recurrent seasonal hunting/fishing settlement in Hekelingen pretty much resemble the distribution of the use wear traces development in Pavlov I.

Tab. 7-22 The distribution of the degree of the development of traces in correspondence with the settlement type. The sites are ordered by the supposed "permanency" of the occupancy.

Degree of the development of use-wear traces	Beek-Molensteeg	Hekelingen III	Pavlov central	Pavlov periphery	DV 1999	Karst
Possible use	39%	63%	60%	36%	55%	80%
Light use	15%	6%	14%	29%	18%	20%
Medium use	15%	14%	19%	28%	27%	0%
Extensive use	31%	17%	7%	7%	0%	0%

Other parameter which seems to correlate with the type/length of the settlement could be the percentage of used retouched pieces (Fig. 7-1). The proportion of all retouched pieces in the assemblage cannot be a representative feature due to same problems with sampling difficulties as it was mentioned for the total percentage of the used pieces in assemblage (above). However, the proportion of the used pieces from the analysed retouched implements could be more resistant to sampling variability.

Tab. 7-23 The percentage of the antler/bone/ivory/wood working traces from the interpreted AUAs.

Excavation	Antler/bone/ivory/wood working
Pavlov central	8%
Pavlov periphery	4%
DV IIa 1999	20%
Karst	0%

In addition, it has been postulated that labour-intensive activities, such as the processing of hides, wood/bone/antler-working, as well as retooling, would indicate long-term or permanent occupation. It is only when people settle for an extended period, that they allocate time for executing such tasks. At short-term camps, briefly visited to exploit a specific resource, all the available time must be devoted to subsistence tasks (Gijn 1990). However, any of the above mentioned worked materials cannot be considered an absolute indicator as the activities have their variations for both short and long term occupations. The relative frequency of these worked materials can suggest the duration of stay; however, this criterion may not enable to differentiate a palimpsest of occupations. In this study this parameter does not reveal any interpretable results (Tab. 7-23). The some correlation between the type of the settlement and the worked material in this study could be seen in hide processing activities, e.g. hide scraping which was detected only in Pavlov assemblage in contrast to the other sites considered as short term occupations.

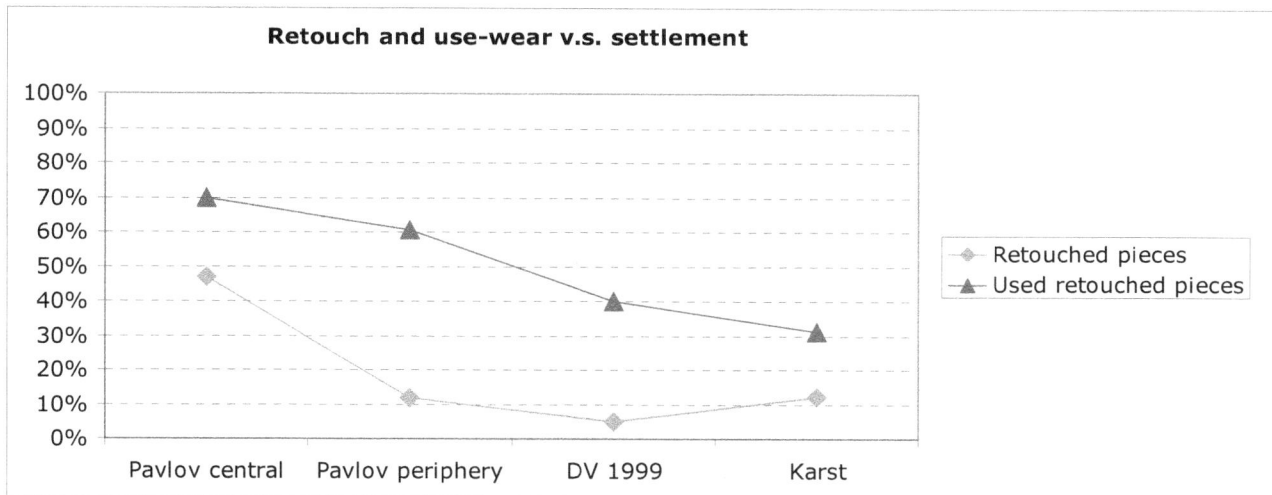

Fig. 7-1 The correlation between the percentage of all retouched pieces and the used retouched tools with the type of settlement. The sites are ordered by the supposed "permanency" of the occupancy.

7.8 Contribution of LPA and HPA to the functional interpretation

As been already mentioned above, trace interpretation was based on both, but separate, LPA and HPA methods. It was expected that the HPA method could contribute only to more precise interpretation of few traces already detected by the LPA method. Nevertheless, HPA was found useful even though the results were provided with lower degrees of certainty than for younger or less patinated assemblages.

Comparison of the results received from LPA and from HPA showed that LPA interpreted only about 40% of analysed artefacts as "used." The remainder of about 60% was interpreted as unsure or not used (Fig 7-2). However, after that HPA was able to further interpret 60% of these unsure LPA traces and about 10% of artefacts originally interpreted by LPA as not used (Fig 7-3). Altogether, that forms about 20% of artefacts, which would not be interpreted by the LPA method. Thus, LPA together with HPA were able to interpret about 60% of analysed artefacts as used. That provided significantly better results than the exclusive use of the LPA method (Šajnerová 2003c).

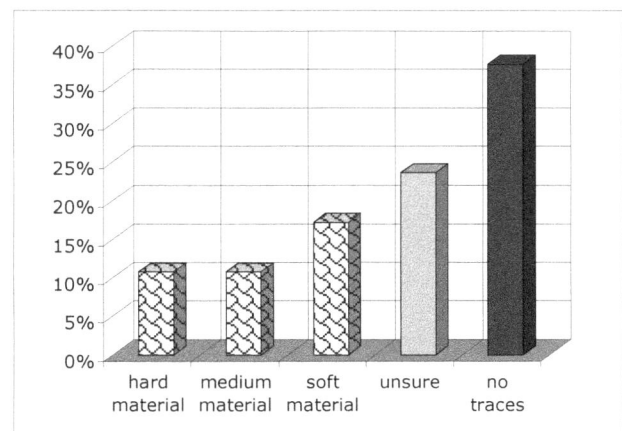

Fig. 7-2 The use-wear traces interpreted using exclusively the LPA method.

Such a result corresponds with the experimental results of e.g. Gijn (1990) where about 27% of experimental tools used for working of hide did not have any traces interpretable by LPA. Micro-chipping is often absent despite the intensive usage. In Vaughan's experiments (1985a) this phenomenon was noted for 16% of tools used in transverse motions and for 18% for those employed in longitudinal motions. As to worked materials, 39% of the edges involving soft contact materials and 6% of those relating to hard materials sustained no microscarring whatsoever (see also Den Dries and Gijn 1997).

The higher percentages of unsure interpretations for LPA in this study are caused by postdepositional rounding of all edges, which could disguise slight rounding from the use. For that reason, the evidence for contact with soft materials such as meat and certain green plants may be absent or underestimated especially in the LPA results.

On the other hand, the LPA method proved to be essential for the interpretation of hard worked materials. The HPA method was able to detect and interpret the use polish only in 30% of the used areas with traces interpreted by LPA as originating from working hard material. Therefore, the interpretation of hard materials based solely on HPA (polishes) would reveal only about one third of traces relating to hard materials.

These results have not brought about any brand new information but they precisely confirmed that the most effective and efficient interpretation of use-wear can be obtained only by using a combination of both methodological approaches, as Keeley in fact already postulated at the beginning of his work. Encouraging news should be that the HPA method should be attempted despite the high age of the analysed assemblage and that it still can provide valuable results for interpreting tool usage.

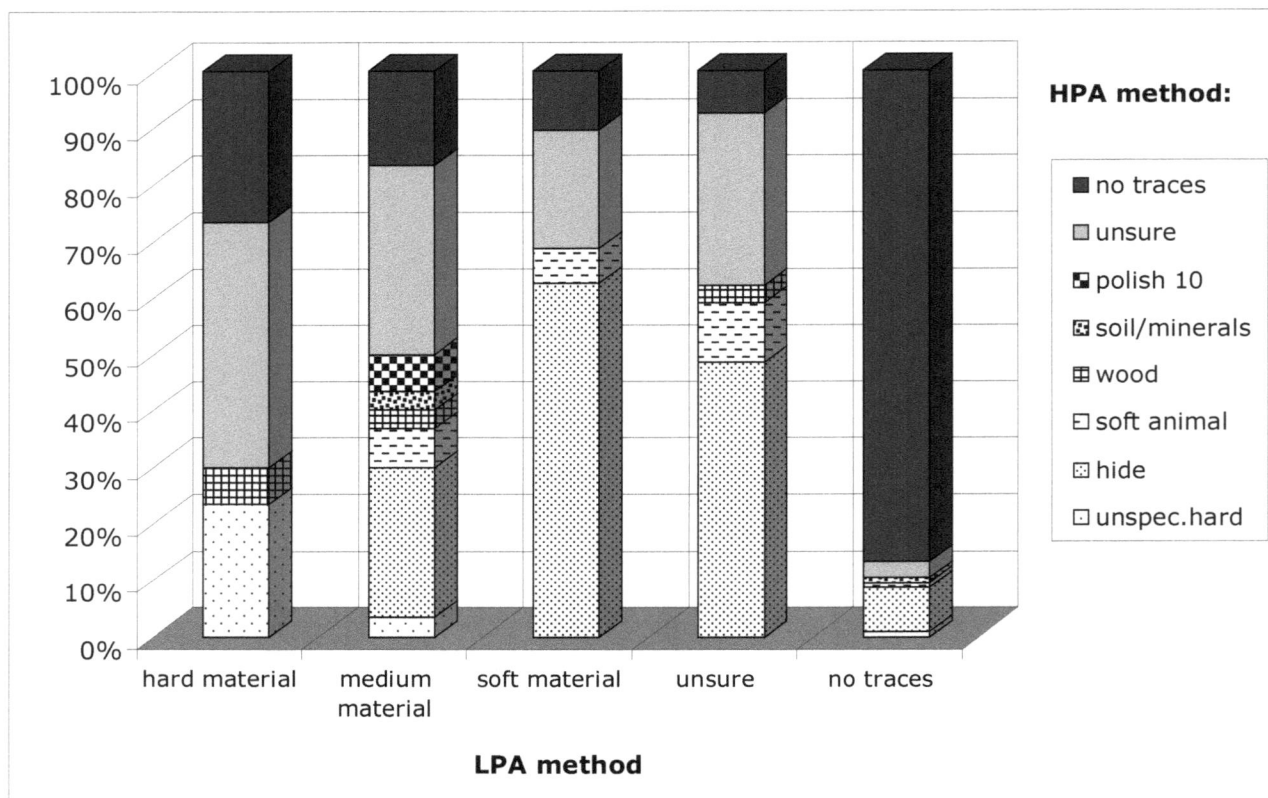

Fig. 7-3 Structure of the interpreted traces using both the LPA and HPA methods.

8. Conclusion

The research proved that microwear analysis is worth performing on patinated Palaeolithic assemblages which generally used to be excluded from microanalyses. The results, although with a lower degree of certainty, are comparable with the other studies performed on more preserved assemblages from younger periods. Despite the patinated material, the application of the HPA method provided the possibility to interpret hide-working traces on the artefacts, which would have left only few traces that might not be detected by the LPA method. However, as this activity seems to dominate the use of the Palaeolithic tools (about 50% of the artefacts were interpreted as used for hide-working), the application of the HPA method provides a significant advantage for interpreting the functions of the tools.

The results of the microwear analysis enable us to shed light on the everyday activities performed by people in the Palaeolithic communities. In accordance with the other studies of Palaeolithic assemblages, hide was interpreted as the predominant material that was worked using the stone tools. However, the results may be exaggerated because the use-wear traces of hide-working have high level of resistance to the postdepositional impacts. The use-wear traces of the hard or medium hard materials were more likely to be interpreted with the use of the LPA method than with the HPA one and therefore the material categories could only be determined roughly. Low percentage of the used microliths and points could be explained by their designated purposes. Points were probably not intended for the extensive use; moreover they are considered to be tools with a short service life. Similar reason could be suggested for the absence of the use-wear traces on microliths, although their purpose in the Gravettian cannot yet be fully explained by microwear analysis.

Traceology further increases the opportunities of the other archaeological method – the spatial analysis (e.g. Bartošíková 2005) – which tries to divide the excavated site into working and living areas, according to the distribution of different types of artefacts, hearths and dwelling structures. The wide range of activities, which were performed at or near the site, can be explored with the use of the functional interpretation of the lithic components from the site assemblage and, thereby, an insight into the function of the site itself can be gained. However, the function of the site cannot be based on the functional data only as the results may omit the non-lithic tools or past removals of the lithic and non-lithic artefacts. Several researchers have demonstrated that the use of microwear analysis together with the spatial analysis and/or the artefacts refitting can serve as powerful instruments when assessing the structure of the site and/or the behavioural aspects of tool manufacturing and usage (e.g. Cahen et al. 1979; Moss 1983a; Dumont 1987; Bartošíková et al. 2003).

I agree with D.T. Price's (1978) idea that microwear analysis should focus more on complete tasks rather than simply on motions and contact materials. In most cases, however, the functional analysis of lithics may at best provide a list of "worked materials" at the various sites unless non-lithic contextual information is provided. The method does not permit the determination if the tool in question was used for complex tasks like fashioning a bow, making a trap or shaping a digging stick. Much of the evidence for such tasks must inevitably come from associated archaeological materials: basically from the survival of the "tasks" themselves. Therefore, close working together of the microanalysts and the archaeologists during the research/microanalysis is necessary, which unfortunately was not fully possible during this study. Thus the complex interpretation of the microwear results could be made only in that basic material-motion level.

Despite its limits, the microwear analysis plays an important role in the Stone Age studies. The method represents the possibility to employ a new approach towards the available (already studied) lithic material. As long as the limits of the interpretation of use-wear traces are kept in mind, valid, valuable and very interesting information can be gained. For the prehistoric periods, for which other types of data records like paintings or scripts are not available, crucial information about the tool functions would otherwise not be possible to obtain.

During the last twenty years, inseparable experimental work which is connected with traceology, together with the application of current ethnographic data, achieved a re-discovery of many of the production techniques and methods common for life in the Palaeolithic and Mesolithic. These techniques and methods demonstrate the ability of our predecessors to survive in difficult natural conditions. They often developed very simple yet effective solutions, which can still be inspiring at present. Therefore, it is without any doubts that this relatively young method is heading for many successive achievements and unthought-of discoveries in the future which will bring us closer to our past.

Acknowledgements

My PhD-research benefited at many points from the perceptive comments and helpful advice of Anne Louise van Gijn and Alexander Verpoorte, my advisors at the University of Leiden. I am most grateful to Jiří Svoboda (Institute of Archaeology ASČR Brno, Research Center for Paleolithic and Paleoethnology in Dolní Věstonice) for the opportunity to participate in their excavations and for the access to the lithic collections for use-wear analysis. Parts of the project would not have been possible without the assistance of a curator of the Hrdlička Museum of Man CU and my PhD supervisor, Božena Škvařilová, who was helping me through difficult periods throughout this research. My thanks also extend to Alfred Pavlik, (University of Tübingen, Germany) for his advice at the early stages of my interest in micro-wear studies.

This research was supported by the Grant Agency of the Charles University under Grant No. 263/1999/B BIO, the Fund of Development of Universities (Ministry of Education, Youth and Sport) under Grant No. 2540/2002, the Czech-Germany Fund for the Future under project No. B/IV/063, grants from The Foundation of Josef, Marie and Zdeňka Hlávkas and the Zonta International.

Further, I would like to thank Alice Lamb and Michelle Jindřichová for language consultation and proofreading. Finally, but most importantly, I am ever so grateful to my husband for his understanding and ongoing support throughout my work and for his courage to put his hands at risk during my experiments.

References

Andersen, H.H., Whitlow, H.J. (1983) Wear traces and patination on Danish flint artifacts. Nuclear Instruments and Methods in Physic Research 218, 468-474.

Anderson, P.C. (1980) A testimony of prehistoric tasks: diagnostic residues on stone tool working edges. World Archaeology 12, 181-194.

Anderson-Gerfaud, P.C. (1981) Contribution méthodologique à l'analyse des micro-traces d'utilisation sur les outils préhistoriques. Thèse de troisième cycle, Universite de Bordeaux, I, n°1607.

Anderson-Gerfaud, P.C. (1986) A few comments concerning residue analysis of stone plant-processing tools. In (Owen L., Unrath G., eds.) Technical Aspects of Microwear Studies on Stone Tools. Early Man News 9/10/11, Tübingen, 69-81.

Anderson-Gerfaud, P.C., Moss, E., Plisson, H. (1987) A quoi ont-ils servi? L'apport de l'analyse fonctionnelle. Bulletin de la Société Préhistorique Francaise 84/8, 226-237.

Bartošíková, Z. (2005) Lithic assemblage of the south-eastern periphery (1957, 1970, 1971). In (Svoboda J., ed.) Pavlov I Southeast. A window into the Gravettian lifestyles. Dolnověstonické studie 14, AÚ AVČR Brno, 112-133.

Bartošíková, Z., Šajnerová, A., Svoboda, J. (2003) Ethnological approach to the site of Pavlov I (Czech Republic). Przeglad Archeologiczny 51, 77-86.

Bettison, J.R. (1985) An experimental approach to sickle sheen deposition and archaeological interpretation. Lithic Technology 14, 26-32.

Beyries, S., Delamare, F., Quantin, J.C. (1988) Tracéologie et rugisimétrie tridimensionnelle. In (Beyries S., ed.) Industries lithiques: traséologie at technologie. Oxford (BAR Int. Ser., 411, vol.2), 115-132.

Binford, L.R. (1982) The archaeology of place. Journal of Anthropological Archeology 1, 5-31.

Bordes, F. (1965) Utilisation possible des Côtés des Burins. Fundberichte aus Schwaben 17, 3-5.

Bordes, F. (1973) Position des traces d'usure sur les grattoirs simple du Perigordien supérieur évolué de Dorbiac (Dordogne). In Estudios Dedicados as Profesor Dr. Luis Pericot, Institutio de Arqueologia y Prehistoria, Universidad de Barcelona, 35-60.

Brink, J. (1978a) Notes on the occurrence of spontaneous retouch. Lithic Technology 7, 31-34.

Brink, J. (1978b) An Experimental Study of Microwear Formation on Endscrapers. Archaeological Survey of Canada 83, Natural Museum of Man: Mercury Series, Ottawa.

Bruijn, A. (1958/59) Technik und Gebrauch der bandkeramischen Feuersteingeräte. Palaeohistoria 6-7, 213-224.

Cahen, D., Keeley, L.H., Van Noten, F. (1979) Stone tools, toolkits and human behaviour in prehistory. Current Anthropology 20(4), 661-683.

Clark, J.D.G. (1975) The Earlier Stone Age Settlement of Scandinavia. Cambridge University Press, Cambridge.

Clark, J.D.G., Thomson, M.W. (1953) The groove and splinter technique of working antler in upper Palaeolithic and Mesolithic Europe. Proceedings of the Prehistoric Society 19, 148-160.

Clarke, D.L. (1976) Mesolithic Europe: the economic basis. In (Sieveking G. de G., Longworth I.H. and Wilson K.E., eds.) Problems in Economic and Social Archaeology. pp. 449-81, Duckworth, London.

Curwen, E.C. (1930) Prehistoric flint sickles. Antiquity 9, 62-66.

Del Bene, T. A. (1979) Once upon a striation: current models of striation and polish formation. In (Hayden B., ed.) Lithic use-wear analysis. New York, 167-178.

Den Dries, M. van, Gijn, A.L. van (1997) The Representativity of Experimental Usewear Traces. In (Ramos-Millán A., Bustillo A., eds.) Siliceous Rocks and Culture, Universidad de Granada, 499-513.

Derndarsky, M., Ocklind, G. (2001) Some Preliminary Observations on Subsurface Damage of Experimental and Archaeological Quartz Tools using CLSM an Dye. Journal of Archaeological Science 28, 1149-1158.

Diamont, G. (1979) The nature of so-called polished surfaces on stone artifacts. In (Hayden B., ed.) Lithic use-wear analysis. New York, 159-166.

Dibble, H.L. (1995) Middle Palaeolithic scraper reduction: Background clarification, and reviews of evidence to date. Journal of Archaeological Method and Theory 2/4, 299-368.

Dumont, J.V. (1982) The quantification of microwear traces: a new use for interferometry. World Archaeology 14, 206-217.

Dumont, J.V. (1983) An Interim Report on the Star Carr Microwear Study. Oxford Journal of Archaeology 2(2), 127-145.

Dumont, J.V. (1987) Mesolithic Microwear Research in Northwest Europe. In (Rowley-Conwy P., Zvelebil M., Blackholm H.P., eds.) Mesolithic Northwest Europe: recent trends. Vol. 2, University of Sheffield.

Dunnell, R.C. (1986) Methodological issues in Americanist artefact classification. In (Schiffe M.B., ed.) Advances in Archaeological Method and Theory. Academic press, New York, 35-99.

Evans, A.A., Donahue, R.E. (2005) The elemental chemistry of lithic microwear: an experiment. Journal of Archaeological Science 32(12): 1733-1740

Evans, J. (1872) The Ancient Stone Implements, Weapons and Ornaments of Great-Britain. D. Appleton and Company, New York.

Finlayson, B., Mithen, S. (1997) The Microwear and Morphology of Microliths from Gleann Mor. In (Knecht, ed.) Projectile Technology. Plenum Press, New York.

Fischer, A., Vemming Hansen, P., Rasmussen, P. (1984) Macro and Micro Wear traces on Lithic Projectile Points. Experimental results and Prehistoric Examples. Journal of Danish Archaeology 3, 19-46.

Flenniken, J.J., Haggerty J.C. (1979) Trampling as an agency in formation of edge damage. North West Anthropological Research Notes 13, 208-214.

Fridrich, J. (1997) Staropaleolitické osídlení Čech. Supplementum PA 10, Praha.

Fridrich, J. (2005) Ecce Homo. Krigl, Praha.

Fridrich, J., Sýkorová, I. (2005) Bečov IV – sídelní areál staropaleolitického člověka ve středozápadních Čechách. Archeologický ústav ČSAV, Praha.

Gendel, P. (1982) Functional analysis of scrapers. In (De Kip , Lauwers R., Vermeersch, eds.) Un Site du

Mesolithique Ancient A Neerharen. Studia Praehistorica Belgica 1, 49-51.

Gijn, A.L. van (1990) The wear and tear of flint. Principles of functional analysis applied to Dutch Neolithic assemblages. Analecta Praehistorica Leidensia 22, Leiden University.

Gijn, A.L. van (1997) Flint. In (Reamaekers D.C.M. et al.) Wateringen 4: A Settlement of the Middle Neolithic Hazendok 3 Group in Duch Coastal Area. Analecta Praehistorica Leidensia 29, Leiden University, 173-182.

Gould, R.A., Koster, D.A., Sontz A.H.L. (1971) The lithic assemblages of the western desert Aborigines of Australia. American Antiquity 36, 149-169.

Grace, R. (1989) Interpreting the function of stone tools. The quantification and computerisation of microwear analysis. BAR Int. Ser. 474, Oxford.

Grace, R. (1996) Use-wear analysis: the state of the art. Archaeometry 38, 2 (1996) 209-229.

Grace, R., Graham, I.D.G., Newcomer M.H. (1985) The quantification of microwear polishes. World Archaeology 17, 112-120.

Grace, R., Graham, I.D.G., Newcomer M.H. (1987) Preliminary investigation into mathematical characterisation of wear traces on flint tools. In (Sieveking G. de G., Newcomer M.H., eds.) The human uses of flint and chert. Cambridge, 63-69.

Hardy, B.L., Kay, M., Marks, A.E., Monigal, K. (2001) Stone tool function at the paleolithic sites of Starosele and Buran Kaya III, Crimea: Behavioural implications. PNAS, Vol.98, No.19, 10972-10977.

Hayden, B. (ed.) (1979) Lithic use-wear analysis. New York.

Hill, J.N., Evans, R.K. (1972) A model for classification and typology. In (Clarke D.L., ed.) Models in Archaeology. Methuen, London, 231-274.

Horáček, I., Ložek, V., Svoboda, J., Šajnerová, A. (2002) Přírodní prostředí a osídlení krasu v pozdním paleolitu a mezolitu. In (Svoboda J., ed.) Prehistorické jeskyně. Dolnověstonické studie 7, ArÚ AVČR Brno, 313-344.

Jahren, A.H., Toth, N., Schick, K., Clark, J.D., Amudson, R.G. (1997) Determining Stone Tool Use: Chemical and Morphological Analyses of Residues on Experimentally

Manufactured Stone Tools. Journal of Archaeological Science 24, 245-250.

Juel Jensen, H. (1982) A Preliminary analysis of blade scrapers from Ringkloster, a Danish Late Mesolithic site. Studia Praehistorica Belgica 2:323-327.

Juel Jensen, H. (1984) A Microwear Analysis of Unretouched Blades from Ageröd V. In (Larsson L., ed.) Ageröd V. An Atlantic bog site in central Scania. Lund (Acta Archaeologica Ludensia, Series in 80 no. 12) 144-152.

Juel Jensen, H. (1986) Unretouched blades in the Late Mesolithic of South Scandinavia. A functional study. Oxford Journal of Archaeology 5(1), 19-33.

Juel Jensen, H. (1988) Functional analysis of prehistoric flint tools by high-power microscopy: review of West-European research. Journal of World Prehistory 2, 53-88.

Juel Jensen, H. (1994). Flint tools and plant working. Hidden traces of Stone Age technology. A use wear study of some Danish Mesolithic and TRB implements. Aarhus University Press.

Juel Jensen, H., Petersen, E.B. (1995) A functional Study of Lithics from Vænget Nord, a Mesolithic Site at Vedbæk, N.E. Sjælland. Journal of Danish Archaeology, Vol. 4, 40-51.

Kamminga, J. (1979) The nature of use-polish and abrasive smoothing on stone tools. In (Hayden B., ed.) Lithic use-wear analysis. New York, 143-158.

Kamminga, J. (1982) Over the edge: functional analysis of Australian stone tools. Occasional Papers in Anthropology 12, University of Queensland, Brisbane.

Kay, M. (1996) Microwear Analysis of Some Clovis and Experimental Chipped Stone Tools. In (Odell G.H., ed.) Stone Tools: Theoretical Insight into Human Prehistory. Plenum Press, New York.

Keeley, L.H. (1974) Techniques and methodology in micro-wear studies: a critical review. World Archeology 5, 323-336.

Keeley, L.H. (1978) Preliminary microwear analysis of the Meer Assemblage. In (Van Noten F., ed.) Les Chasseurs de Meer. Dessertationes Archaeologica Gandenses 18, De Tempel, Brügge, 73-86.

Keeley, L.H. (1980) Experimental determination of stone tool uses. A microwear analysis. University of Chicago Press, Chicago.

Keeley, L.H. (1981) Premiers resultants de l'analyse des microtraces d'utilisation de quelque objects. In (Audouze F., Cahen D., Keeley L.H. and Schmider B.) Le Site Magdalenian du Buisson Campin à Verberie (Oise). Galia Préhistoire 24 (1), 137-41

Keeley, L.H. (1982) Hafting and retooling: Effects on the archeological record. American Antiquity 47(4), 780-809.

Keeley, L.H. (1987) Hafting and retooling at Verberie, In (Stordeour D., ed.) La main et l'outil. Lyon (Traveaux de la Maison de l'Orient, 15), 89-96.

Keeley, L.H., Newcomer, M.H. (1977) Microwear analysis of experimental flint tools: a test case. Journal of Archaeological Science 4, 29-62.

Keeley, L.H., Toth N. (1981) Microwear polishes on early stone tool from Koobi Fora. Kenya. Nature 293, 464-465.

Klíma, B. (1956) Statistická methoda - pomůcka při hodnocení paleolithických kamenných industrií, Památky archeologické XLVII, 193-210.

Klíma, B. (1957) Výzkum paleolitického sídliště u Pavlova v roce 1954, Archeologické rozhledy 9, 145-151, 177-184.

Klíma, B. (1995) Dolní Věstonice II: ein Mammutjägerrastplatz und seine Betattungen. ERAUL 73/Dolnověstonické studie 2, Liège.

Knutsson, K. (1988a) Patterns of tool use. Scanning electron microscopy of experimental quartz tools. AUN 10, Societas Archaeologica Upsaliensis, Uppsala.

Knutsson, K. (1988b) Making and using stone tools, the analysis of the lithic assemblages from Middle Neolithic sites with flint in Västerbotten, Northern Sweden. AUN 11, Societas Archaeologica Upsaliensis, Uppsala.

Knutsson, K. (1998) Convention and lithic analysis. In (Holm L., Knutsson K., eds.) Proceedings from the Third Flint Alternatives Conference at Uppsala, Sweden, October 18-20, 1996. Occasional Papers in Archaeology 16.

Larsson, L. (1983) Ageröd V. An Atlantic Bog Site in Central Scania. Acta Archeologica Ludensia, Series in 8° No.12.

Levi-Sala, I. (1986) Use wear and post depositional surface modification: a word of caution. Journal of Archaeological Science 13, 229-244.

Levi-Sala, I. (1988) Processes of polish formation on tool surface. Beyries 1988 Vol. 2, 83-98.

Levi-Sala, I. (1993) Use-wear traces: processes of development and post-depositional alternations. ERAUL 1993 Vol.2, 401-416.

Levi-Sala, I. (1996) A study of Microscopic Polish on Flint Implements. BAR International Series 629, Oxford.

Malina, J. (1980) Archeologie včera a dnes. České Budějovice.

Mansur, M.E. (1983) Scanning electron microscopy of dry-hide-working tools: the role of abrasives and humidity in microwear polish formation. Journal of Archaeological Science 10, 223-230.

Mansur-Franchomme, M.E. (1983) Traces d'utilisation et technologie lithique: examples de la Patagonie. (Thesis) Bordeaux.

Meeks, N.D. Sieveking, G. de G., Tite M.S., Cook, J. (1982) Gloss and use-wear traces on flint sickles and similar phenomena. Journal of Archeological Science 9, 317-340.

Minta-Tworzowska, P. (1994) Klasyfikacja w archeologii. Poznań.

Mortensen, P. (1970) A preliminary study of the chipped stone industry from Beidha, an Early Neolithic village in southern Jordan. Acta Archaeologica 41, Copenhagen, 1-54.

Moss, E.H. (1983a) The Functional Analysis of Flint Implements. Pincevent and Pont D'Ambon: Two Case Studies from the French Final Paleolithic. BAR, International Series 177, Oxford.

Moss, E.H. (1983b) Some comments on edge damage as a factor in functional analysis of stone artifacts. Journal of Archaeological Science 10, 231-242.

Moss, E.H. (1986) What microwear analysts look at. In (Owen L.R., Unrath G., eds.) Technical aspects of microwear studies on stone tools. Tübingen, 91-96.

Moss, E.H. (1987a) A review of 'Investigating microwear polishes with blind tests'. Journal of Archaeological Science 14, 473-481.

Moss, E.H. (1987b) Polish G and the question of hafting. In (Stordeur D., ed.) La main et l'outil, Lyon (Travaux de la Maison de l'Orient 15), 97-102.

Moss, E.H., Newcomer, M.H. (1982) Reconstruction of Tool Use at Pincevent: Microwear and Experiments. Studia Praehistorica Belgica 2: 279-287.

Movius, H. (1968) Note on the history of the discovery and recognition of the function of burins in tools. In Prèhistoire: Problèmes et Tendances. Paris, 311-318.

Musil, R. (2005) Animal prey. In (Svoboda J., ed.) Pavlov I Southeast. A window into the Gravettian lifestyles. Dolnověstonické studie 14, AÚ AVČR Brno, 190-228.

Newcomer, M.H. (1974) Study and replication of bone tools from Ksar Akil (Lebanon). World Archaeology 6, 138-153.

Newcomer, M.H., Grace, R., Unger-Hamilton, R. (1986) Investigating microwear polishes with blind tests. Journal of Archaeological Science 13, 203-218.

Odell, G.H. (1975) Microwear in perspective: a sympathetic response to Lawrence H. Keeley. World Archaeology 7, 226-240.

Odell, G.H. (1977) The application of microwear analysis to the lithic component of an entire prehistoric settlement: methods, problems and functional reconstruction. (Thesis) Harvard University, Harvard.

Odell, G.H. (1980) Butchering with stone tools: some experimental results. Newsletter of Lithic Technology 9, 39-48.

Odell, G.H. (1981) The morphological express at functional junction: searching for meaning in lithic tool types. Journal of Anthropological Research 37, 319-342.

Odell, G.H., Odell-Vereecken, F. (1980) Verifying the reliability of lithic use wear assessments by blind tests: the low-power approach. Journal of Field Archaeology 7, 87-120.

Plew, M.G., Woods J.C. (1985) Observation of edge damage and technological effects on pressure-flaked stone tools. In (Plew M.G., Woods J.C., Pavesic M.G., eds.) Stone tool analysis. Essay in honour of Don C. Crabtree. Albuquerque, 211-228.

Plisson, H. (1982) Analyse Fonctionelle de 95 micro-grattoirs "Tourassiens". Studia Praehistorica Belgica 2:278-287.

Plisson, H. (1986) Alterations des micropolis d'usage: quelques experiences complementarires. In (Owen L.R., Unrath G., eds.) Technical aspects of microwear studies on stone tools. Tubingen, pp.111-116.

Plisson, H., Mauger, M. (1988) Chemical and mechanical alteration of microwear polishes: an experimental approach. Helinium 28/1, 3-16.

Price, D.T. (1978) Mesolithic settlement systems in the Netherlands. In (Mellars P., ed.) The Early Postglacial Settlement of Nothern Europe. Duckworth, London, 81-113.

Rigaud, A. (1972) La Technologie du Burin appliqué au Matériél Osseux de la Garenne (Indre). Bulletin de la Société Préhistorique Française 69, 104-108.

Rigaud, A. (1977) Analyses typologique et technoloque des grattoirs magdaléniens de la Garrone à Saint-Marcel (Indre). Gallia Préhistoire 20, 1-43.

Rosenfeld, A. (1971) The examination of use marks on some Magdalenian endscrapers. The British Quarterly 35, 176- 182.

Roebroeks, W., Kolen, J., Poecke, M., Gijn, A.L. van (1997) Site J: An Early Weichselian (Middle Palaeolithic) Flint Scatter at Maastricht-Belvedere, The Netherlands. Paleo 9, 143-172.

Rots, V. (2003) Towards and Understanding of Hafting: The macro- and microscopic evidence. Antiquity 77 (298), 805-815.

Rots, V. (2004) Prehensile Wear on Flint Tools. Lithic Technology 29 (1), 7-32.

Rottländer, R. (1975a) The formation of patina on flint. Archaeometry 17, 106-110.

Rottländer, R. (1975b) Some aspects of patination on flint. Staringia 3, 54-56.

Seitzer Olausson, D. (1980) Starting from Scratch: The History of Edge-Wear Research from 1838 to 1978. Lithic Technology IX/2, 48-60.

Semenov, S. (1957) Pervobytnaja technika. Materialy i Issledovania po Archeologii SSSR 54, Nauka, Moskva – Leningrad.

Semenov, S. (1968) Rozvitie techniky v kamennom veke. Nauka, Leningrad.

Shea, J.J. (1988) Methodological consideration in affecting the choice of analytical techniques in lithic use-wear analysis: tests, results and application. In (Beyries S., ed.) Industries lithiques: traséologie et technologie. BAR Int. Ser., 411, vol.2, Oxford, 65-82.

Shepherd, W. (1972) Flint. Its origin, properties and uses. London.

Schmalz, R.F. (1960) Flint and the patination of flint artefacts. Proceeding of the Prehistoric Society 26, 44-49.

Schulte im Walde, T., Strzoda, U. (1985) Zur Funktion der modifizierten Klingen aus Siggeneben-Süd - ein Bispiel für ihren Gebrauch im Frühneolitikum. Offa 42, 243-260.

Sonnenfeld, J. (1962) Interpreting the function of primitive implements. American Antiquity 28, 56-65.

Spurrell, F.C.J. (1892) Notes on early sickles. Archeological Journal 49, 53-69.

Stapert, D. (1976) Some natural surface modification on flint in the Netherlands. Palaeohistoria 18, 7-42.

Straus, L.G. (2002) Selecting Small: Microlithic Musings for the Upper Paleolithic and Mesolithic of Western Europe. In (Elston R.G, Kuhn S.L., eds.) Thinking Small: Global Perspectives on Microlithization. Archeological Papers of the American Athropological Assotiation 12, 69-82.

Svoboda, J. (1987) Stránská skála. Bohunický typ v brněnské kotlině. Studie Archeologického ústavu ČSAV v Brně XIV/1, Academia Praha.

Svoboda, J. (ed.) (1991) Dolní Věstonice II – western slope. ERAUL 54, Liège.

Svoboda, J. (ed.) (1997) Pavlov I – Northwest. Dolnověstonické studie 4, Brno.

Svoboda, J. (1999) Čas lovců. Brno.

Svoboda, J. (2000) Brno-Stránská skála (k.o. Slatina, okr. Brno-město). Přehled výzkumů 40, 147-149.

Svoboda, J. (2003) Bohunician and Aurignacian Typology at Stránská skála. In (Svoboda J., Bar-Yosef O., eds.) Stránská skála. Origins of Upper Palaeolithic in the Brno basin, Moravia, Czech Republic. American

School of Prehistoric Research Bulletin 47, Dolnověstonické studie 10, Harvard University.

Svoboda, J. (2005) Pavlov I – Southeast. Location, stratigraphy, microstratigraphies and features. In (Svoboda J., ed.) Pavlov I Southeast. A window into the Gravettian lifestyles. Dolnověstonické studie 14, AÚ AVČR Brno, 25-52.

Svoboda, J., Bar-Yosef, O., eds. (2003) Stránská skála. Origins of Upper Palaeolithic in the Brno basin, Moravia, Czech Republic. American School of Prehistoric Research Bulletin 47, Dolnověstonické studie 10, Harvard University.

Svoboda, J., Valoch, K. (2003) History and Strategy of Research at Stránská skála. In (Svoboda J., Bar-Yosef O., eds.) Stránská skála. Origins of Upper Palaeolithic in the Brno basin, Moravia, Czech Republic. American School of Prehistoric Research Bulletin 47, Dolnověstonické studie 10, Harvard University, 167-171.

Symens, N. (1986) A functional analysis of selected stone artifacts from the Magdalenian site of Verberie, France. Journal of Field Archaeology 13 (1), 213-222.

Šajnerová, A. (2001) Trasologická analýza štípané industrie z naleziště Dolní Věstonice IIa (výzkum 1999). Památky archeologické XCII/1, 158-164.

Šajnerová, A. (2003a) Use-wear analysis. In (Svoboda J., Bar-Yosef O., eds.) Stránská skála. Origins of Upper Palaeolithic in the Brno basin, Moravia, Czech Republic. American School of Prehistoric Research Bulletin 47, Dolnověstonické studie 10, Harvard University, 167-171.

Šajnerová, A. (2003b) Mikoskopická analýza staropaleolitických artefaktů z lokality Stránská skála I. Acta Mus.Moraviae, Sci. soc. LXXXVIII, 67-73.

Šajnerová, A. (2003c) Use-wear analysis of Moravian Palaeolithic chipped industry. Anthropologie XLI/1-2, 49-54.

Šajnerová, A. (2005) Use-wear analysis of the lithics. In (Svoboda J., ed.) Pavlov I Southeast. A window into the Gravettian lifestyles. Dolnověstonické studie 14, AÚ AVČR Brno, 134-147.

Texier, P.J. (1981) Désilification des silex taillés. Quarternaria 23, 159-169.

Tomášková, S. (1991) Use-wear Analysis of the Lithic Material from Dolní Věstonice, Czechoslovakia. In (Svoboda J., ed.) Dolní Věstonice II - Western slope. ERAUL 54, 97-101, Liège.

Tomášková, S. (1994) Use-wear analysis and its spatial interpretation. In (Svoboda J., ed.) Pavlov I excavations 1952-1953. Eraul 66/Dolnověstonické studie 2, Liège, 28-40.

Tomášková, S. (2000) The Nature of Difference: History and Lithics at Two Upper Paleolithic Sites in Central Europe. BAR, International Series 880, BAR Publishing, Oxford.

Tomášková, S. (2003) Nationalism, local histories and the making of data in archaeology. Journal of Royal Anthropological Institute (N.S.) 9, 485-507.

Tomášková, S. (2005) What is a Burin? Typology, Technology, and Interregional Comparison. Journal of Archaeological Method and Theory 12 (2), 79-115.

Tringham, R., Cooper, G., Odell, G., Voytek, B., Whitman, A., (1974) Experimentation in the formation of edge damage: a new approach to lithic analysis. Journal of Field Archaeology 1, 171-196.

Unger-Hamilton, R. (1984) The formation of use-wear polish on flint: beyond the deposit versus abrasion controversy. Journal of Archeological Science 11, 91-98.

Unger-Hamilton, R. (1985) Microscopic striation on flint sickle-blades as an indication of plant cultivation: Preliminary results. World Archaeology 17, 121-126.

Unrath, G., Owen, L.R., Gijn, A.L. van, Moss, E.H., Plisson, H. et al. (1986) An evaluation of microwear studies: a multi-analyst approach. In (Owen L.R., Unrath G., eds.) Technical aspects of microwear studies on stone tools, Tübingen, 117-76.

Valoch, K., Šajnerová, A. (2005): Les fouilles du site du Paleolithique Inferieur de Stranska Skala IA Brno-Slatina. BAR, Int. Ser. No. 1364, Oxford, 370-385.

Vaughan, P. (1985a) Use-wear analysis of flaked stone tools. Tucson.

Vaughan, P. (1985b) The burin-blow technique: Creator or eliminator? Journal of Field Archeaeology 12, 448-496.

Verpoorte, A. (2001) Place of Art, traces of fire. A contextual approach to anthropomorphic figurines in the Pavlovian (Central Europe, 29-24 kyr BP). Archaeological Studies Leiden University 8, Leiden.

Verpoorte, A. (2005) The lithic assemblage of Pavlov I (1954, 1956, 1963, 1964). In (Svoboda J., ed.) Pavlov I

Southeast. A window into the Gravettian lifestyles. Dolnověstonické studie 14, AÚ AVČR Brno, 75-111.

White, J.P., Modjeska, N., Hipuya, I. (1977) Group definitions and mental templates: an ethnographic experiment. In (Wright R.V.S., ed.) Stone tools as cultural markers: change, evolution and complexity. New Jersey, 380-390.

Whitthoft, J. (1967) Glazed polish on flint tools. American Antiquity 32, 383-388.

Yamada, S. (1993) The formation process of 'use-wear polishes'. ERAUL 1993 Vol. 2, 433-445.

Yamada, S., Sawada, A. (1993) The method of description for polished surfaces. ERAUL 1993 Vol. 2, 447-457.

www.ingramcontent.com/pod-product-compliance
Lightning Source LLC
Chambersburg PA
CBHW051306270326
41926CB00030B/4746